CW00515242

MOTORCYCLES

WHITE STAR PUBLISHERS

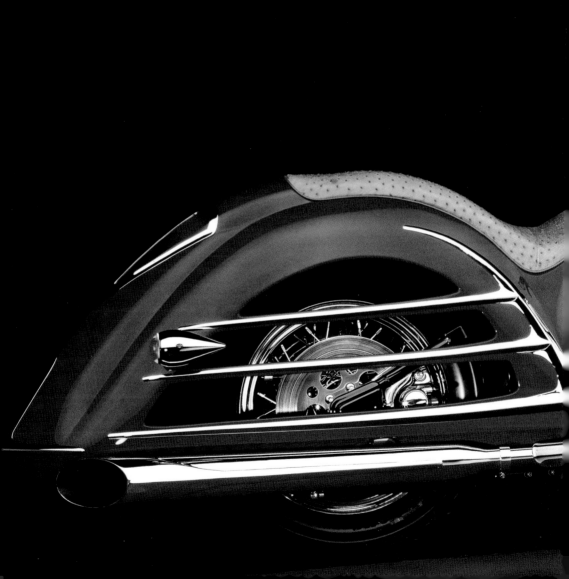

EDITED BY

VALERIA MANFERTO DE FABIANIS

editorial coordination
LAURA ACCOMAZZO

text by
ENZO RIZZO

graphic design
CLARA ZANOTTI

graphic layout
MARIA CUCCHI

translation
DAVIDE LAMAGNI

© 2007 WHITE STAR S.P.A.
VIA CANDIDO SASSONE, 22-24
13100 VERCELLI - ITALY
WWW.WHITESTAR.IT

- The Piaggio Vespa, here in the GTS sport version.

ISBN 978-88-544-0271-3

REPRINTS:
1 2 3 4 5 6   11 10 09 08 07

Printed in Singapore

CONTENTS

MOTORCYCLES

1 • Indian: the dawning of the motorcycle.

2-3 • 1939 Harley Davidson.

4-5 • Custom Chrome Classic Fl Shovelhead Profile of 1979.

6-7 • Valentino Rossi watching Nicky Hayden at the Spanish GP trials of Moto GP 2006.

8-9 • Harley Davidson dressed in red: it's a Bob Dron Heritage Royal Red of 1992.

10-11 • Indian Scout from 1930.

15 • Riff Raff Orange Flames, a 2003 custom bike.

16-17 • A very "muscular" custom–this is a Steroid bike.

18-19 • This Harley's gas tank is like a sculpture on two wheels.

20-21 • Nicky Haiden at the Laguna Seca GP valid for the Moto GP 2006.

22-23 • The start of the 2006 Enduro du Touquet.

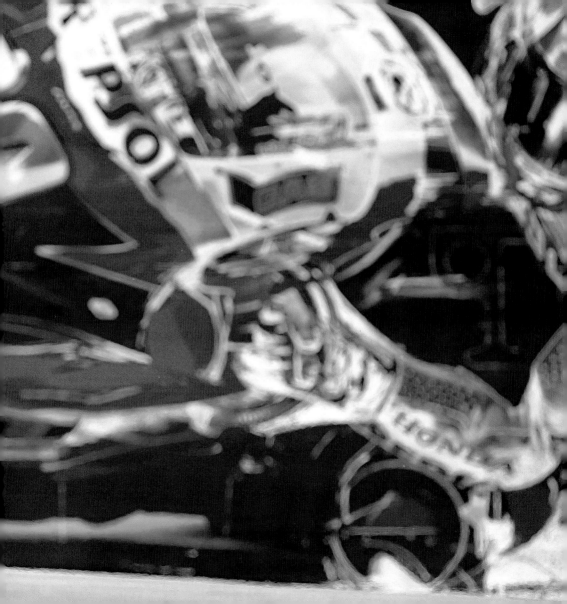

Introduction

Motorcycles are generators of passion. And not only for easy rider style bikers or for those wanting to feel the thrill of speed in the pursuit of that sense of freedom which is often missing inside of us. It is a way of being, which has seduced art, conquered cinema, inspired literature with concepts and techniques going beyond the characteristics of the mechanical object. The evolution of the motorcycle engine represents the first sign of wealth of a peoples, where individuals may not be able to afford a car as a private means of travel: do not be surprised, therefore, if you will see even three people riding a bike

- Besides the funny text, this motorcycle fully represents the spirit of Miami, and Ocean Drive is its street.

Introduction

IN CHINA, INDIA, VIETNAM OR MONGOLIA. YOU MIGHT EVEN SEE WHOLE FAMILIES ON ONE MOTORBIKE, OR EVEN PEOPLE CARRYING HUGE LOADS WITH THEM. IN ALL THESE CASES YOU WILL SEE THE SATISFACTION OF RIDING A MOTORBIKE IN THEIR EYES, NOT SO DIFFERENT FROM THE EXPRESSION OF THE DEDICATED BIKER OR RACETRACK DRIVER. MOTORCYCLES ARE ALSO A RITUAL: GETTING DRESSED, ACCURATELY PREPARING THE SUIT, BOOTS, WIND STOPPER, HELMET, READY TO TACKLE THE ASPHALT AND SMELL IT. A RITE WHICH MAKES NO DISTINCTION BETWEEN AGE, SEX OR RACE: THOSE WHO THINK THIS BELONGS ONLY TO THE MALE WORLD ARE MAKING A MISTAKE. THE GENTLE SEX HAS INCREASED ITS MOTORCY-

Introduction

CLING PRESENCE WITH THE RETURN OF SCOOTERS, EASI-
ER TO DRIVE AND USE BY AN EXCLUSIVELY URBAN TARGET.
NOT ONLY: SCOOTERS HAVE ALSO RE-LAUNCHED THE MO-
TORCYCLE MARKET, WHICH WAS GASPING AT THE END OF
THE 90S. HOW SATISFYING FOR THE ICON OF THESE MOD-
ELS, THE STAINLESS VESPA, A YOUNG AND SPARKLING 60-
YEAR-OLD WHICH REVOLUTIONIZED THE WAY PEOPLE
RIDE. TO THIS DAY THERE HAS BEEN NO EASING IN ITS SUC-
CESSFUL CAREER. NOW THERE ARE THE MAXI-SCOOTERS,
IDEAL FOR LONG JOURNEYS: THEY HAVE BROUGHT NEW
PEOPLE TO MOTORCYCLING, EVEN THOUGH THERE ARE
DETRACTORS AMONG HARD AND PURE MOTORCYCLISTS.
FOR THEM, THESE ARE NOT MOTORBIKES. YOU DON'T

Introduction

STRADDLE A SCOOTER BUT YOU SIT ON IT AS IF IT WERE AN ARMCHAIR. AND FORGET ABOUT LEANING INTO BENDS... THE HISTORY AND SUCCESS OF MOTORCYCLING IS TIED TO ITALY NOT ONLY BECAUSE IT INVENTED THE SCOOTER: IT WAS ALSO PROTAGONIST IN THE BIRTH OF PRODUCTION COMPANIES AND COMPETITIONS. IN THE PAST AS TODAY ITS MODELS AND PILOTS, AT THE BEGINNING OF THE THIRD MILLENNIUM, DOMINATE THE WORLD MOTORBIKE RACING CIRCUS.

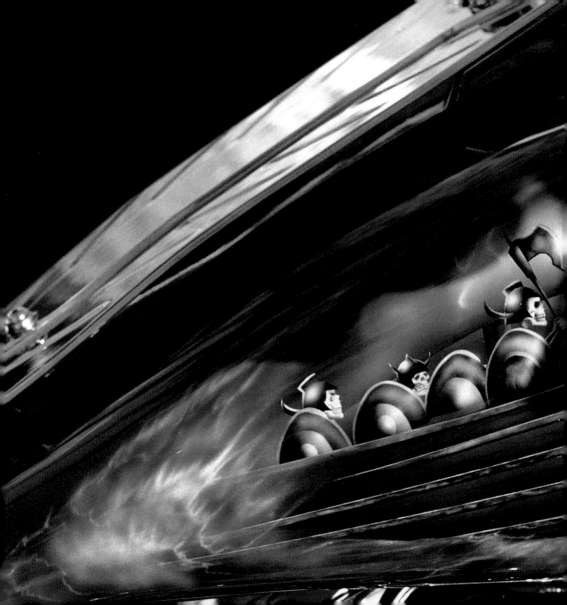

The ORIGINS of the MYTH

Seen today, the similarity of this first Harley Davidson of 1903 with a bicycle makes one smile.

INTRODUCTION The Origins of the Myth

IT IS RATHER SWEET TO SEE BLACK AND WHITE PICTURES AND FADED FILMS OF MOTORCYCLE PIONEERS, MUSTACHIOED GENTLEMEN IN THEIR SUNDAY BEST, CLUMSILY SHOWING OFF THEIR INVENTION, GIVING DEMONSTRATIONS THAT OFTEN LED TO RUINOUS FALLS DUE TO PRECARIOUS BALANCE. NOT TO MENTION THE FIRST MODELS WHICH BETRAYED THEIR KINSHIP TO BICYCLES AND THEIR VELOCIPEDE ANCESTORS, THE LATTER BEING A KIND OF BICYCLE WITH PEDALS AS THE MAIN MEANS OF PROPULSION BUT WITH A MOTOR WHICH COULD BE ENGAGED ON COMMAND. THE MOTORCYCLE WAS INVENTED MORE THAN A CENTURY AGO, BUT CONSIDERING THE TECHNICAL PROGRESS THAT HAS BEEN MADE, IT'S AS IF TEN CENTURIES HAVE GONE BY. ITS EVOLUTION SWEPT AWAY

INTRODUCTION The Origins of the Myth

BRANDS THAT MADE IMPORTANT CONTRIBUTIONS TO THE HISTORY OF THE MACHINES, BEFORE BEING LOST IN TIME, VICTIMS OF SUDDEN CHANGES AND INEVITABLE DECLINE. BUT WHO CAN DEFINE MR. MOTORCYCLE? AT THE END OF THE 19TH CENTURY, THANKS TO THE INVENTIVENESS OF FRENCHMAN GEORGES BOUTON, THE FIRST MOTORIZED TRICYCLE WAS BORN, FOLLOWED SOON AFTERWARDS BY A MOTORIZED TWO-WHEEL VEHICLE. THE RUSSIAN WERNER BROTHERS INVENTED THIS, AND THEY CALLED IT A "MOTORCYCLETTE". THE FIRST WITH A SPARK-IGNITION ENGINE WAS INVENTED BY TWO GERMAN INVENTORS, GOTTLIEB DAIMLER AND WILHELM MAYBACH, WHO LATER BECAME FAMOUS FOR AUTOMOBILES. THEY MADE THE FIRST PROTOTYPE IN 1885 IN A SMALL WORKSHOP IN CANNSTATT,

The Origins of the Myth

CLOSE TO STUTTGART. FRENCH INVENTOR LOUIS-GUIL-LAUME PERREAUX OBTAINED HIS FIRST PATENTS IN 1868, AND IS CONSIDERED ANOTHER FORERUNNER WITH HIS STEAM-POWERED VEHICLE. BEFORE THE END OF THE 19TH CENTURY, THE FIRST WORKING MODELS WERE ON SALE; FROM THEN ON, THE INEXORABLE EVOLUTION OF MOTOR-CYCLES TOOK OFF IN THE WHOLE WORLD, ESPECIALLY IN EUROPE AND IN THE UNITED STATES. UNTIL THE 1960'S, PRODUCTION MAINLY TOOK PLACE IN EUROPE, WITH ITAL-IANS, THE ENGLISH AND GERMANS AT THE FOREFRONT. THEN THE JAPANESE ARRIVED, MONOPOLIZING THE MAR-KET AND LEADING IT EVER SINCE.

The 70s sport motorcycle was like this Norton 750 Pr: windshield, a modeled seat and few extras.

46 • This is the first motorbike made in the USA, and it has three wheels like the Orient Trike of 1900 made in Brooklyn with the French De Dion-Bouton engine.

47 • The first Harley Davidson of 1903 had a De Dion mono-cylinder 400 cc engine.

48 • This Gilera of 1909 already had a colored tank: also notice the long transmission belt.

49 • Splendid in its red fairing, this Pierce Arrow of 1910 made in the USA had a straight-4 engine.

50-51 ● Ever more a motorbike and less a bicycle: here is the Indian Racer of 1912 complete with luggage rack.

52-53 ● A decade from the first model, the evolution of the Harley Davidson can be seen in this 1914 model.

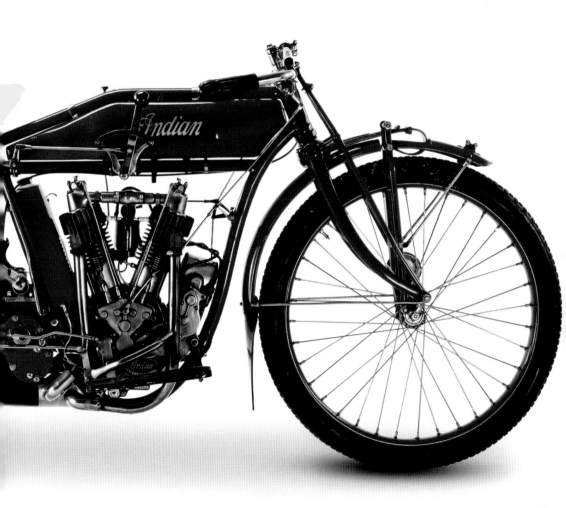

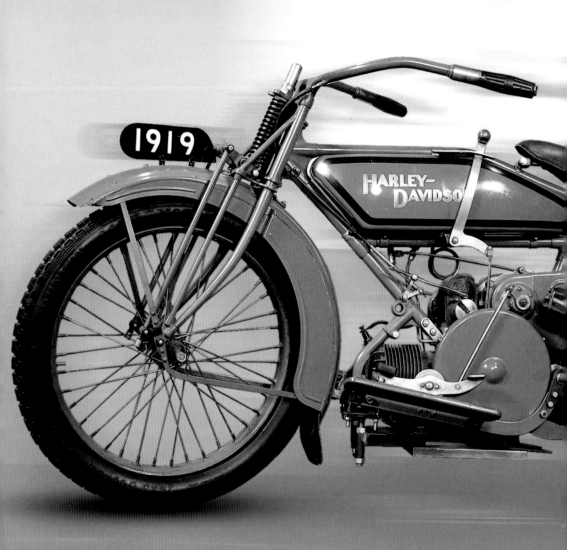

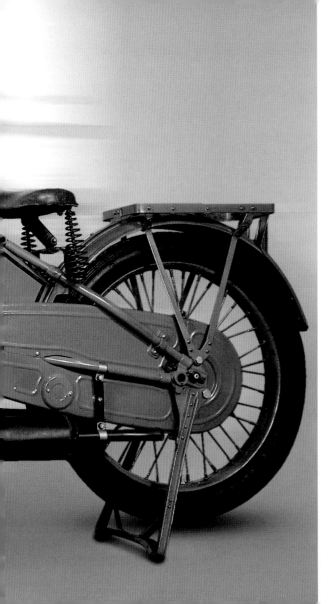

- With a power of 6 horses this Harley Davidson Sport Twin of 1919 reached 50 mph and cost 335 dollars.

56 • There is also a small light on this Triumph Model H of 1916, made during the war.

57 • A 500 cc engine for this Moto Guzzi Normale 500 produced between 1921 and 1924.

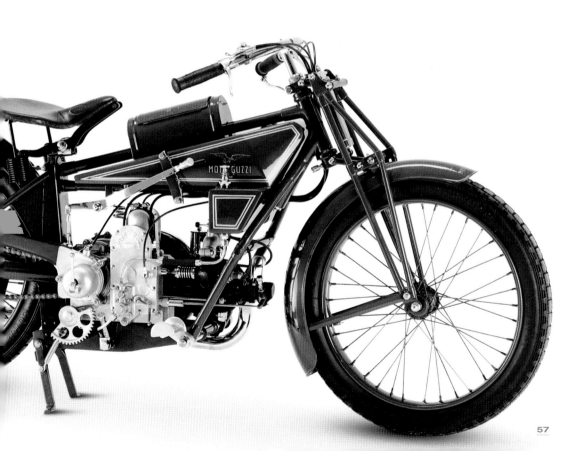

58-59 ● At Benelli's they also think of the fairer sex: here is the Motoleggera 125 Donna of 1924.

59 ● The large anterior betrays its inclination for travel: it is the Benelli 175 Turismo of 1928.

A red fairing but black light and horn for this Indian Scout of 1925: it had a 600 cc engine.

62 • Tanks start reaching important dimensions as shown by this Indian Prince of 1928.

62-63 • First customizations with well-refined rear bags of excellent making for the 1927 Indian Ace.

64-65 ● A researched and usual red fairing for the Gt Norge 500 Moto Guzzi of 1929.

65 ● Of a more sporting and essential set up than the Norge was the Moto Guzzi C4V.

Not only bicycles for the Italian maker Bianchi as demonstrated by this 175 Freccia d'Oro (Golden Arrow, seen on the tank) of 1930.

Splendid in its complete chroming, fairing included; Ducati Corsa N.5–see the practically nonexistent seat.

● Splendid with its
bicolor chromate tank:
the Bianchi S500V,
made in 1935.

72 • Essential and researched in its profile and the form of its tank, this is a French Motosacoche of 1932.

72-73 • The ancient ivory of the chassis, from the fenders to the tank, exalt the clean elegance of a rare Ollearo of 1947.

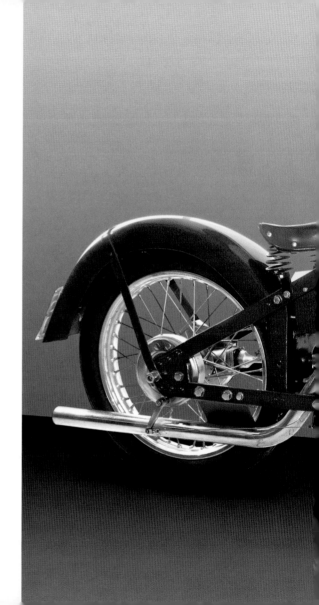

74 ● This Sertum dates back to the mid 30s; it is equipped with a two-cylinder 500 cc engine.

74-75 ● From Denmark comes this Nimbus 750 of 1934: the straight-4 engine is unique.

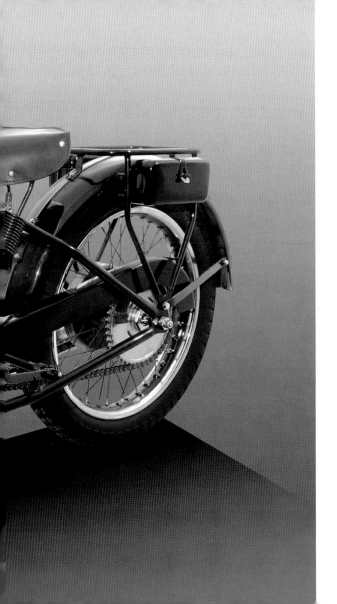

● Tricolor cockade
and researched style
with mini rear bags.
It is a Della Ferrera VT
of 1935.

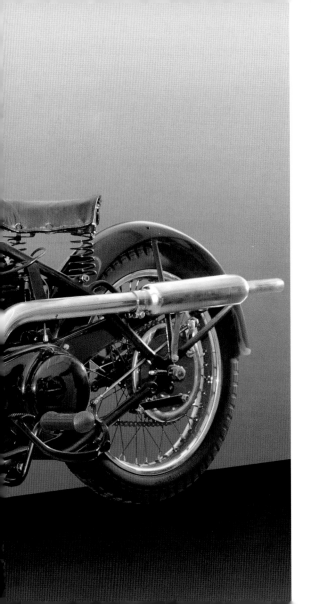

78-79 ● This Miller 500 Sv5
of the mid 30s has peculiarly
shaped exhausts.

79 ● Another Miller, of 1932, with
a lower capacity, seeing this
model's denomination is 175.

80 • The Norton 500 VT of 1938 had a
mono-cylinder engine but a two-cylinder
one would fit also.

81 • From Benelli comes this 250 cc model
good for long journeys but only solo.

82 • The typical mark of Harley Davidson can be seen in this El of 1939.

82-83 • Another bicolor Harley but this time in white and blue: it is the U of 1938.

84 • This Benelli 500 VI dressed
in black with long exhausts
dates from 1940.

84-85 • This elegant pre-war
Benelli bears witness to the many
Italian motorcycle producers in the
first part of the 20th century.

86-87 • Many customs and this Harley Davidson Fl of 1941 already has a well defined personality.

87 • The lights are tripled, the chroming extended: this is the Ulh Harley Davidson of 1941.

88-89 • War time coloring and accessories for this Military Indian of 1941.

Refined in its finishing, as the decoration on this tank and the bags show on this Indian Model 741 of 1943.

92 ◦ This two-seater Harley Davidson F of 1946 was made right after the war.

92-93 ◦ Military version with front rifle carrier for this Harley Davidson XA produced in 1942.

94 ● A brilliant color and
extensive chroming for this Harley
Davidson Fl of 1947.

94-95 ● A very elegant custom
in its color and wheels with white
band, it is a 1942 Harley Davidson.

Made for competition, with a space for the race number; here we have a Benelli 250.

98 ● This BMW 500 Corsa of 1955 is of a
racing nature: see the tiny windshield and
space for race number.

99 ● A BMW motorcycling classic: this is
an R51 with two-cylinder boxer engine.

100 • A sporting style, long saddle and big tank for the Rumi 125 Junior.

101 • Even this Classic Velocette has a sporting slant with a front lateral space for the race number.

● Original and visionary was this fairing with windshield, a Royal Enfield Airflow of 1951.
The instruments highlight two big indicators and a smaller one further up.

104-105 • A Moto Guzzi classic in the usual red: a Falcone, here with a 500 cc engine.

105 • Still a Guzzi but here is a Bicilindrica, a two-cylinder with an engine of 500 cc.

Checkered wheels for off-road use for this compact BSA Gold Star produced in 1954.

Observe the studied set up with decorated tanks and bags of this 50s Indian.

110-111 • More sober in the set up compared to the usual, this is the Harley Davidson FI made in 1951.

111 • Shocking pink and typical Harley Davidson set up for this FLH of 1955.

112 • Elegant in its black and gray fairing, a Norton produced in the 50s..

112-113 • Aerodynamic research besides aesthetics: this is the streamlined Norton N93 made for competition.

114-115 • Airplanes or motorcycles for the Italian Aermacchi, it makes no difference: here is the elegant Chimera of 1956.

115 • Yet another Aermacchi but this time it is the end of the 50s (1959): this is the Ala Verde 250.

116 ● From the early 50s comes this AJS 500, a sober tourism motorcycle.

116-117 ● This AJS 650 SS shows more study compared to the models of ten years earlier. It is 1962.

It rewards the eye and is dedicated to those with a strong sense of aesthetics, this Ducati Apollo in cream color, of 1963.

120 • Very sporting with a highlighted tank
and slight tank, this is a Gilera 9 of 1963.

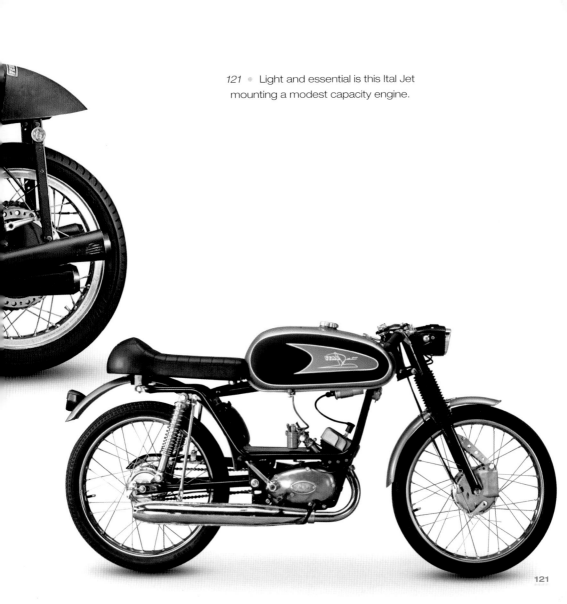

121 • Light and essential is this Ital Jet
mounting a modest capacity engine.

In the 60s BMW launched the R69S with the successful boxer engine.

124 • This Honda CB450 of 1965 would still be in demand today seeing the return of classic road models.

124-125 • The Honda CB750 Four from 1969 is an icon of high-powered road bikes, very popular in the 70s.

A road model but with a sporting inclination, this is a Ducati MK3 with a single cylinder engine of 350 cc.

128 • A road vehicle with enduro aspirations, this is a Honda 450 CL of the late 60s.

129 • No frills but elegance in this Suzuki T500, made in 1967.

A model which could
easily be sold today
seeing the current
production: this is
the Norton
Commando 750.

132-133 • The BSA A65 Spitfire of the 60s is another legendary "Made in England" motorcycle, much sought after by collectors.

133 • The BMW R75/5 of 1969's design is still valid today and is quite in demand by collectors.

134 • Essential and sporty, the Laverda SF750 of 1972: today it would be a high performance naked.

134-135 • For connoisseurs and with a truly original sporting coat, this is the MV Agusta 750 Sport of 1973.

● Born for competition,
this Ducati 500 GP 1971
has a pronounced
aerodynamic fairing.

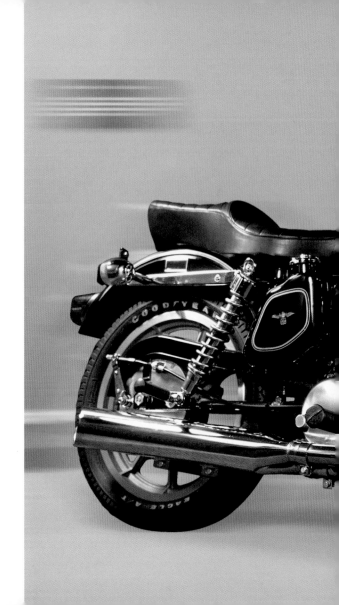

A very slender and dynamic Harley Davidson: it is an HDL1000 in a splendid black and gold coat.

RIDING
a DREAM

● Advertising poster for the 1929 Triumph: the bike races off with a simple blow.

INTRODUCTION Riding a Dream

To EASILY UNDERSTAND THE EVOLUTION AND HISTORY OF MOTORCYCLES ALL YOU NEED TO DO IS LOOK AT ADVERTISING.

YES, THAT'S RIGHT; POSTERS, BILLBOARDS AND EVERYTHING THAT NOW COMES UNDER THE TERM ADVERTISING HAS BEEN THE BEST REFLECTION OF THE TIMES FOR MOTORBIKES.

ADVERTISING HAS ALWAYS GIVEN AN EXACT IMAGE OF THE DAILY USE OF MOTORBIKES, WHETHER IN NEW YORK, ROME, PARIS, LONDON OR SYDNEY.

ADVERTISING, ESPECIALLY ON BILLBOARDS, IS WITHIN EVERYONE'S REACH, EVEN MORE SO THAN CINEMA, FOR THE VERY REASON THAT IT IS ON THE STREETS. MANY ARTISTS FROM ALL OVER THE WORLD HAVE

INTRODUCTION Riding a Dream

LENT THEIR TALENTS AND CREATIVITY TO THE ADVER-
TISING OF THE MORE FAMOUS BRANDS, BUT ALSO TO
SPORTING AND TOURIST EVENTS TIED TO THE WORLD
OF MOTORCYCLES, SO BIKES HAVE BECOME A POPU-
LAR IMAGE.

THROUGH THEM, ONE CAN TRACE CHANGES
IN THE GRAPHIC STYLE AND IMAGES HIGHLIGHTING
THE POLITICAL, SOCIAL, ECONOMICAL AND CULTURAL
CLIMATE IN THE BACKGROUND OF THE TIME.

ADVERTISING DESIGN HAS REPRESENTED SPORT
EVENTS AND FASHION MORE THAN ART, THEN, FROM
THE ART NOUVEAU NYMPHS AND CHARACTERISTIC
MYTHOLOGICAL HEROES TO THE PHOTOGRAPHIC RE-
ALISM IN THE YEARS OF THE EUROPEAN ECONOMIC

Riding a Dream
Introduction

RENAISSANCE AFTER WWII, AND ITS ABSTRACT SILHOU-
ETTES OF FUTURIST DESIGN.

THE SCOOTER BOOM AT THE END OF THE 90'S WAS GIV-
EN A FURTHER BOOST BY OPENING UP TO THE YOUNG
AND TO THE FAIR SEX. THE FEMALE FIGURE, IN PARTIC-
ULAR, HAS NOW CHANGED SIDES: OFTEN USED AS A
PROVOCATIVE FIGURE ON MOTORCYCLES TO SEDUCE
BIKERS, OR, IN EARLIER TIMES, OFTEN RELEGATED TO
THE ROLE OF PASSENGER ON SUNDAY TRIPS, POR-
TRAYED SITTING SIDE-SADDLE WITH A FLOWING HEAD-
SCARF, WOMEN ARE NOW FINALLY TARGETS OF ADVER-
TISING CAMPAIGNS. AND NOT JUST FOR SCOOTERS.

- The brand is already an icon, as shown by this Vespa advertisement
from 1955 by Raymond Savignac.

146 • A very glamorous 1900 lithography for the British James, sovereign of bikes and motorbikes.

147 • More than a poster, this billboard for the Parisian Motocycles Comiot is a work of art.

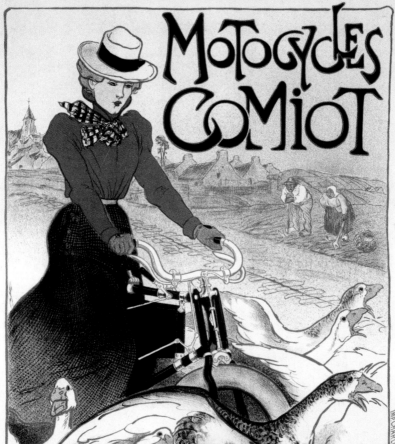

148 • This 1906 poster by Robert Guzarl for the French Terrot is acrobatic and brightly colored.

149 • A 1897 country poster for Peugeot by Valentigney.

Peugeot ~Valentigney
(DOUBS)

IMP. G. ELLEAUME, 10, Rue de Buci, PARIS

REPRÉSENTANT :

Thor

IMP. G. ELLEAUME_10, Rue de Buci - PARIS

FFON"

France has always distinguished itself for its creativity in motorcycle advertising, even on three wheels.

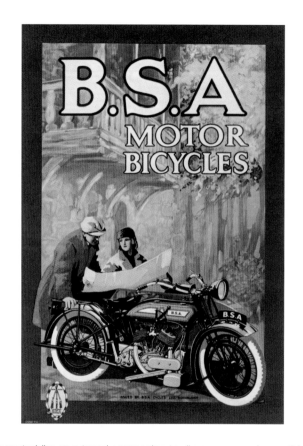

152 • The motorbike as a travel companion to discover new places: this is already the case for B.S.A. in 1926.

153 • Impeccable on the saddle of this 1905 Griffon.

"Griffon"

154 ● Him, on his motorbike, rushing to her, on a bicycle: both are Terrot models on this 1938 poster.

155 ● Technical characteristics are already at the forefront: it is 1913.

THE FLYING MERKEL

The Only Motorcycle in the World With A Self-starter & Two-Speed Gear

J.P. Schomm Crossing
the Great American
Desert on his Flying
Merkel Motorcycle

156 ⬦ This Munich Automobile
Club billboard of 1930 is based
on speed.

156-157 ⬦ An original competition
bike: Germany 1910.

158 • This stylized poster was made by Marcello Nizzoli for a 1929 Moto Sacche model.

159 • Another Nizzoli for this Fabrique Nationale d'Armes de Guerre advertisement of 1925.

160 • The English Norton, always at the top, with a sidecar and ready for big journeys: it's 1932.

161 • He, she, and the requisite motorbike for a picnic excursion: this is the German
Victoria motorbike portrait (1928).

VICTORIA
Motorräder

Verkaufstelle:

Josef Mayr, München

Thalkirchnerstrasse 66/70 / Fernsprecher 55136 und 57593

162 • The fastest motorcycle in the world: sportiness has always been in BMW's DNA, here in a 1930 poster.

162-163 • This Matchless poster of 1939 is based on the concept of speed.

CHLESS

Cycles 1939

de la belle m

CYCLES FAVO

anique!

Bellenger 37

MOTOS

_164-165_ • Beautiful mechanics much appreciated by specialists: it is a poster of the late 30s.

_165_ • This poster by Rene Vincent of 1905 is funny and entertaining.

166 • Who said that motorbikes can be only driven by men? For Gilera it isn't so...

167 • Victory in competitions is always the best possible publicity for bikes as shown by a 1951 MV poster.

MILANO-TARANTO 1951, 1400 Km.

ANCHE QUEST'ANNO LE **MV** 125
STRAVINCONO NELLA CORSA DI VELOCITA' E RESISTENZA
PIU' LUNGA DEL MONDO, ARRIVANDO I II III IV V

168 • Another formidable image accosts women and motorbikes in 1950.

169 • A German advertising poster for the Horex Regina sidecar of 1955.

170 • Brigitte Bardot poses for a motorbike advertisement.

171 • 1950 Lambretta Innocenti advertisement.

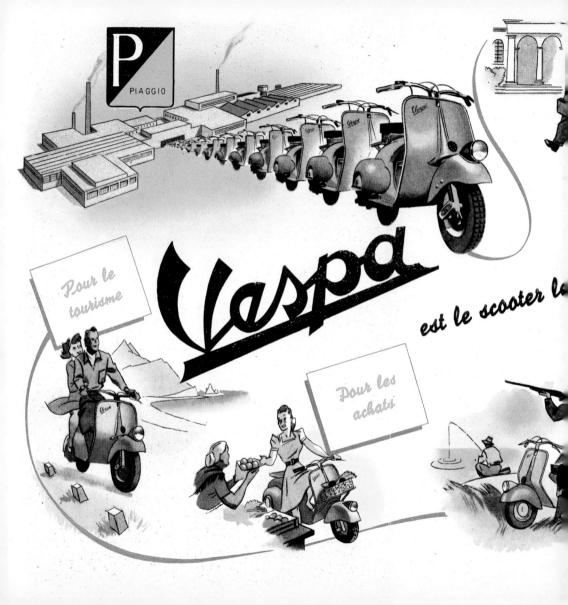

ARIEL *The Modern*

SF 39

Motor Cycle

172-173 ● The world of Vespas is truly great and the French know it too, as shown by this poster.

174-175 ● This Ariel advertisement dates back to 1950.

176 • Even the Pesaro Motobi bets on the woman-motorbike couple.

177 • The Gilera 125 can be driven blindfolded, often with the fairer sex as protagonist. It's 1949.

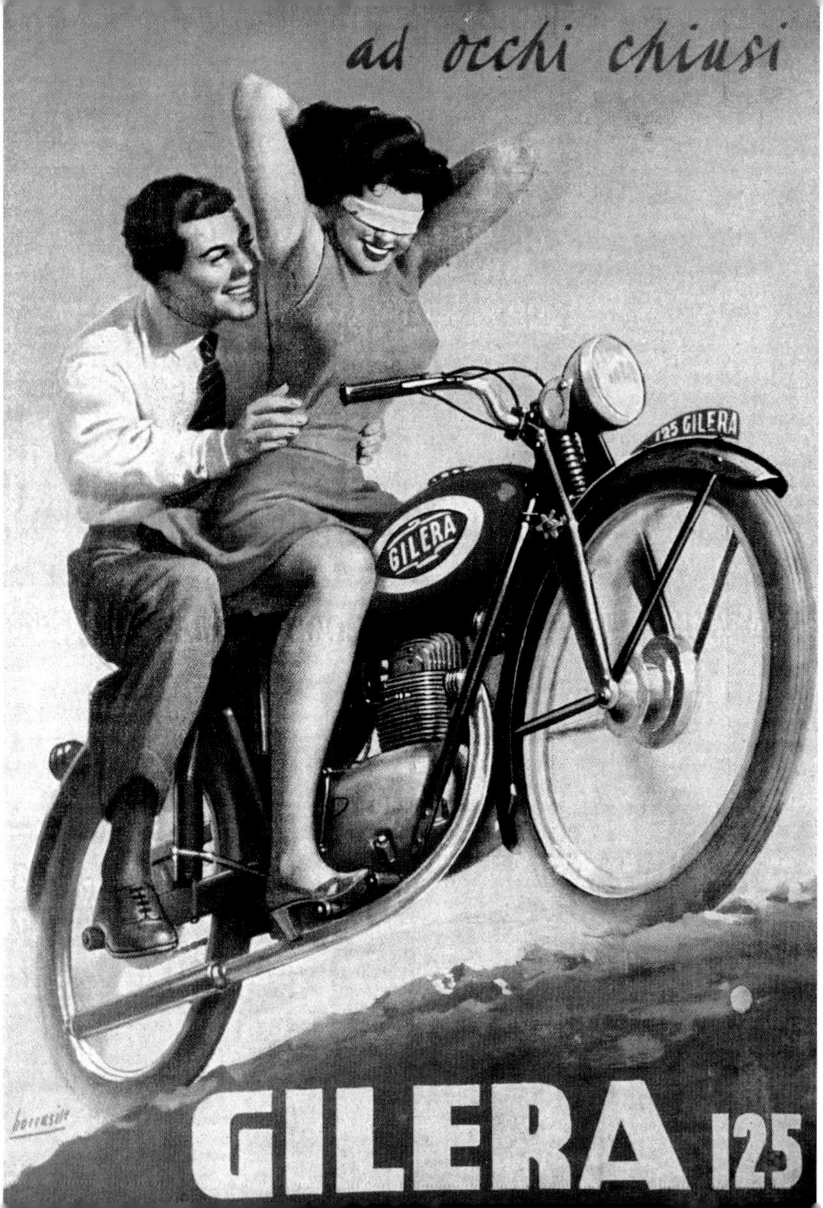
ad occhi chiusi
125 GILERA
GILERA
GILERA 125

178 • A flirtatious advertisement with a woman waving from a Vespa Piaggio: it's an advertising postcard of 1950.

179 • A seaside version for the appreciation of men in this 1950 Vespa poster.

The ROAD QUEENS

- Grand Prix atmosphere and official racing red for the Ducati 999. Pure sport.

INTRODUCTION The Road Queens

ADORED, WORSHIPPED, SANCTIFIED. CALL THEM STARS, LEGENDS, PHENOMENA, SOME MOTORCYCLES WENT BEYOND THE HISTORY OF TWO-WHEEL VEHICLES TO WHICH THEY CONTRIBUTED ENORMOUSLY. WITH THEIR PERSONALITY, DICTATED BY FORM, DETAIL, MECHANICS AND AESTHETICS, THEY CONVEYED EMOTIONS THAT CODIFIED A LIFESTYLE AND A WAY OF BEING WHICH COMPLETELY DOES AWAY WITH SOCIAL STATUS. TAKE HARLEY DAVIDSONS FOR EXAMPLE: THESE ARE GENERALLY RECOGNIZED AS LEGENDARY MOTORBIKES. FROM A PURELY MECHANICAL AND STRUCTURAL POINT OF VIEW THEY MAY DISAPPOINT FANS OF MECHANICS AND PERFORMANCE, BUT MODELS SUCH AS THE MILWAUKEE HAVE A SOUL, AS WHOEVER HAS OWNED ONE KNOWS.

INTRODUCTION The Road Queens

HARLEYS HAVE ALWAYS BEEN THAT WAY, EVER SINCE BROTHERS ARTHUR AND WALTER DAVIDSON BEGAN MAKING THEM IN THEIR GARDEN SHED WITH THEIR FRIEND WILLIAM HARLEY BACK IN 1903. THEY ARE A SYMBOL OF FREEDOM, WHICH MORE THAN ANY OTHER EMBODIES THE DESIRE TO TRAVEL, ESCAPE, RUN AWAY, A SHOUT OF JOY LET OUT TO THE WORLD, LIKE THE UNMISTAKABLE RUMBLE COMING OUT OF THEIR EXHAUST PIPES. IT IS NOT A QUESTION OF FASHION BUT OF A WAY OF BEING, NOT JUST FOR BIKERS IN STUDDED LEATHER JACKETS RIDING ON EVERY HIGHWAY, BUT FOR DREAMERS TO GET LOST IN A DREAM WHICH SOON COMES TRUE. AND NOT ONLY HARLEYS ARE AMONG THE LEGENDS: WE MUSTN'T FORGET THE AUSTRIAN KTM, AN OFF-

The Road Queens
Introduction

ROAD ICON, AS WELL AS THE JAPANESE HONDA, SUZUKI AND KAWASAKI; THE BRITISH TRIUMPH; THE OTHER AMERICANS, BUELL AND INDIAN, OR THE CROWDED ITALIAN GROUP WITH DUCATI, MV AGUSTA, MOTO GUZZI, CAGIVA, APRILIA, MONDIAL AND PARILLA. LEGENDS OF YESTERYEAR WHICH WERE MAINLY BORN OUT OF COMPETITIONS, THEY WERE THE MASTERS OF SPEED AND FATHERS OF LEGENDARY CHARACTERS. AND IN THE PRESENT, THERE IS A BRAND THAT SPEAKS THE LANGUAGE OF MUNICH, GERMANY. IT IS BMW, ANOTHER HISTORICAL BRAND THAT NOW MORE THAN EVER IS CATALYZING RECENT HISTORY AND BETTING ON THE FUTURE OF "STEEL HORSES".

- This Suzuki GSXR is a road model, but it wouldn't look out of place on the race track, either.

186 • The other face of the Ducati, for promenades, in warm and elegant colors: it is the GT 1000.

186-187 • The Ducati GT 1000 betrays a classic line which has come back into fashion in the Third Millennium.

188 • This Ducati Paul Smart 1000 Limited Edition lives for the elegance of its chrome indicators on a white background.

189 • The fairing and the big round light give a vintage air to the modern Ducati Paul Smart 1000 Limited Edition.

A legend in its classic black fairing and rigid bags: here is the Harley Davidson Electra Glide.

192 ● The copper color characterized this European-build road bike legend: it is a BMW R90S of 1975.

192-193 ● The BMW R80 GS: robust, not too powerful but unstoppable. It is the German response to the Japanese enduros.

194 • The Yamaha XT500 of
1975 was a trampoline for the 600
cc version, an icon of enduros.

194-195 • A classic of the
late 70s: it is a Yamaha XS-650
Sport of 1979.

196 ● The Laverda 1200 of 1977 is the Italian response to the Japanese machines of the 70s.

197 ● The Laverda 125 with a Zundapp engine was a dream for the 70s youngsters.

Sophisticated and even with a little windshield, this Honda CBX 1000 F II of 1981 was comfortable for two people even on long trips.

200 • A rather sober fairing for the Harley Davidson Sportster 1000 betrays its US origins.

201 • Muscular, aggressive, wild, with a really small back wheel: this is the
Harley Davidson Special Nera.

202-203 • The Moto Guzzi California, here in the Mark II, 1000 version of 1982, is a custom which interprets in its own manner the Harley overseas.

203 • The Moto Guzzi Le Mans 850 is an absolute legend of the 80s, the symbol of velocity and of "Made in Italy".

A little racy, a little for tourism, this is a single-seater Laverda RGS 1000 of 1981.

A refined outline with a streamlined and bony shape. This is the injection Suzuki 1100i of 1981.

The Honda Gold Wing G l 1500 of 1988 is a limousine on two wheels with radio, air conditioning and leather seat.

This Aprilia Af1 125 Sintesi of 1988 has a full chassis and double front light.

This Japanese bike
is inspired by the Harley
Davidson: it is the
Yamaha V-Max,
a re-birth in design.

The name of this model speaks of the philosophy behind it: the Cagiva Mito (legend) in a splendid fairing.

216 • This high performance Kawasaki 500 GPZ, is seen here in a full red fairing, ad hoc for long trips.

216-217 • This Kawasaki GPZ of 1995 has a 1100 cc engine.

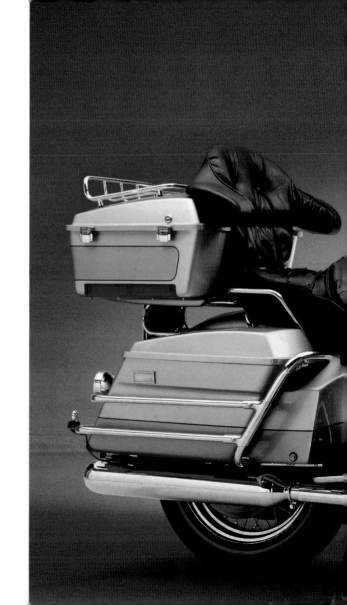

Classy and elegant, this is a Harley Davidson Genuine Classic: notice the attention for passengers and the big luggage case and rack.

This BMW K1 has a futuristic shape, a 1000 cc boxer engine and ABS, it's a rarity among motorbikes.

222 • The Suzuki R 1100 GSX is rather slight in its white and azure full fairing.

222-223 • The Suzuki GSX R with 1100 engine combines performance and elegant design.

The Honda CBR900 RR Fireblade of 1993 is pure speed and color sophistication.

226 • A classic 90s road bike is the Yamaha Diversion 900 of 1994 with integrated windshield.

227 • The Ducati Monster 900 is a naked icon, a pioneer in its category and point of reference in the 90s.

An enduro which would be hard to recognize if it weren't for the brand on the tank: it's a Moto Morini 9/12.

This is the motocross, the KTM, here in the 250 EXC version with a snazzy yellow body.

• Exclusivity on two wheels: it's the Yamaha Virago 535 dressed by the luxury designer, Hermès.

234 • The Suzuki GSX R in the classic white red and blue dress sport also
extended to the fairing.

235 • The Aprilia Motò designed by Philippe Starck made bikes into design objects.

236 • This Triumph SPM has very low exhausts.

237 • The Triumph TBird is refined in its set-up and in the variety of coloring.

237

It has a classic line but in truth it's Italian: it's the Cagiva Raptor 650.

● Essential, a collector's designer model: it's a Moto Morini 9/12 here in a red variant with chromed inserts on the tank.

Enfolding, refined in its orange tonality and the decoration which runs along the tank and the back: it's a Harley Davidson V Rod.

● This is the model
which introduces the
world of Harley
Davidson, the 883,
a true symbol of the
US brand.

The Senna 1000, named after the famous Formula 1 driver, shows its elegance and sportiness. Like the Brazilian driver.

The union of two very distant worlds from a motorcycling point of view: it's a Triumph America, simple and essential.

Elegant, aggressive and classically BMW, The K1200 GT can be seen here in a splendid dark coat.

With personality, no frills, for those who love bikes in their essence: here is the Triumph Speed Triple of 2005.

• For lovers of enduros, this is the goal: the BMW R1150GS, easy to handle and dynamic with a German flavor.

256-257 • This 'baddie' is for real experts. The Buell Firebolt XB9R is a racing bike disguised as a road vehicle.

257 • The name suggests the inclination towards long trips even if it is just for one passenger and is not too comfortable: here is the Buell XBb12X Ulysses.

258 • Aggressive, and not only
due to the integral fairing, the
Honda CBR 600 F is velocity in its
purest form.

258-259 • Elegant and powerful
engine of large capacity and
big brake disks: it's the Honda
CB 1300.

A vaguely vintage flavor and classically British spirit are the essence of the Triumph Bonneville T100.

262-263 • The Yamaha TDM is an enduro with high performance, with an aggressive front and a very slender line.

263 • The Yamaha Xj900 is a classic road model with few frills except for the colored bands.

264 • Chassis in full view, uncolored: the Suzuki SV1000S, is a very aggressive naked..

264-265 • The 650 cc version of the Suzuki SV: like the 1000, fairings and windshields are banished.

266-267 ● More refined and gentler than we had been used to with the KTM, this is the Lc4 640 Adventure.

267 ● KTM also briefly ventured into enduro territory with this 950 Super Enduro.

268-269 • Evil and super fast with its complete fairing in red and black, this is a Yamaha Yzf-R6.

269 • The Yamaha Xj600 S Diversion: very classic as a faired sports model, it is slightly older than the Yzf-R6 to the left.

● An aggressive name,
perhaps excessive for
this kind of bike: it's the
Kawasaki Eliminator 125.

A front with typical Japanese pointed windshield: this is the Suzuki V-Strom.

274 • A suggestive view from the handlebars of this Ducati Sport 1000.

275 • This might look like a Japanese grand tourism model, but in truth it's "Made in Italy": Ducati Sporttouring St3.

The Aprilia Etv 1000 Caponord is an enduro which has long journeys in its DNA, offering comfort and robustness.

An extravagant coloring
but in tones which recall
the Kawasaki colors:
it's an Z750.

Not only extreme sports models but also very aggressive naked bikes: it's the Mv Agusta Brutale Oro.

282 • The color changes but it is still capable of stunning in its chrome shine; a Kawasaki Z 750.

283 • Another variation on the Kawasaki Z 750 theme, in shades of black and gray.

Very Harley in its shapes but also in the chrome and well designed arrangement: it's a Triumph Rocket III.

● Black, elegant, almost austere, but of certain charm with a classical English aplomb: it's a Triumph Speedmaster.

The BMW K 1200 has a sporty livery with an whole fairing and a daringly German coloring.

Fit for coast-to-coast rides and comfortable for two: it's the Kawasaki VN 1600 Classic Tourer.

Shiny and with a sapient touch of orange in the chassis and the seat, this is the Mv Agusta Brutale S.

More simplified, without bags or windshield, this is a less dressed version of the Kawasaki VN 1200 Classic.

The Moto Guzzi Breva 850 abandons the 'company' red for a classic an elegant black.

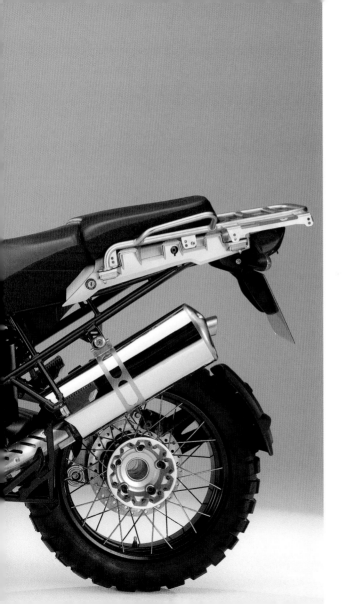

This BMW R1200 is a version ready for off the road with ample protections and checkered tires.

Shiny and completely faired, this Harley Davidson V Rod comes form the Third Millennium.

A portrait of an Italian wild bike: it's the MV Agusta F4, 1.000 cc and a lot of grit.

It's sporty but not disappointing for long journeys: here is the BMW K1200 R Sport.

Also available in capacities below the liter, the 1600 la Kawasaki Vn900 Classic, which shows off its robust exhausts. Notice the detail of the single element instrument panel.

The GSX R 750 is a timeless sporty bike with an off beat livery for a Suzuki.

This Suzuki is "urban" and modern and has its indicators integrated into the tank.

311

An all-black naked of a very aggressive posterior: it's the Suzuki Sv650 with an exposed chassis.

313

314 ● This Japanese custom is a Suzuki Intruder VZ800 K7 inspired by Harley Davidsons.

314-315 ● An imposing machine with a car's engine capacity: it's the Intruder M1800R, a racy custom with generous exhausts.

● The Suzuki GSX-R
750 (in this case the
2003 model) has a
more than twenty-year
brilliant career: it was
1985 when it began to
burn the roads.

• The Ducati Multistrada 1100 is a motorcycle with a special design as shown by the windshield. Its back exhausts are also above the optical group.

This Bimota is called Delirio and it looks like an assembled bike characterized by the color of its chassis tubes well in evidence..

On the EDGE of SPEED

- Not even the rain can stop Valentino Rossi on his victorious Yamaha at the England GP 2005 in Donington.

INTRODUCTION On the Edge of Speed

TRUE, RACE TRACKS ARE AN EXPRESSION OF SPEED, BUT FOR MOTORCYCLES THEY ARE A LITTLE MORE: RACES ON TRACKS ARE MORE FASCINATING FOR MOTORCYCLES THAN WITH CARS, WITH DRIVERS' KNEES GRAZING THE TARMAC ON CURVES AND GROUPS OF BIKES RACING AT NEARLY 200 MPH JUST A FEW INCHES APART AS IF THEY WERE ONE; THAT'S HOW CLOSE THEY ARE. A TRULY UNIQUE SHOW, WITHOUT CONSIDERING TRI-AL COURSES OR SPEEDWAY RACES ON ELLIPTICAL ICE, SAND OR ASH TRACKS. THEN THERE ARE GRASS TRACKS ON OVAL CIRCUITS, ESPECIALLY POPULAR IN GREAT BRITAIN AND AUSTRALIA, AND SIDECARS, WITH A SECOND PILOT IN THE CAR, STABILIZING THE VEHICLE. THE 1907 TOURIST TROPHY ON THE ISLE OF MAN IS THE AUTHORI-

INTRODUCTION On the Edge of Speed

TATIVE MOTORCYCLE COMPETITION BENCHMARK, EVEN IF FRANCE AND ENGLAND HAD ALREADY FOUGHT IT OUT FOUR YEARS EARLIER WITH 3000 CC BIKES (THE FRENCH WON AT AN AVERAGE SPEED OF 55 MPH.). THE WORLD CHAMPIONSHIP DEBUTED IN 1949 WITH BIKES DIVIDED INTO CLASS 125 CC, 250 CC, 350 CC, 500 CC AND SIDECAR. ITALIAN PRODUCERS DOMINATED: GILERA, BENELLI, GUZZI, MORINI, DUCATI, LAVERDA, GARELLI, MOTOBI, MONDIAL AND MV AUGUSTA. IN THE 1960'S THE JAPANESE ARRIVED (HONDA, SUZUKI, YAMAHA AND KAWASAKI) WITH CHAMPIONS LIKE MIKE HAILWOOD AND GIACOMO AGOSTINI. IN THE 80'S AND 90'S US DRIVERS (ROBERTS, SPENCER, LAWSON, RAINEY AND SCHWANTZ) AND AUSTRALIAN ONES (GARDNER AND DOOHAN) WERE UNBEAT-

On the Edge of Speed

ABLE, ESPECIALLY IN THE 500 CC CLASS. THE WORLD CHAMPIONSHIP IS THE MOST WATCHED AND LOVED MOTORCYCLE EVENT, AND MOTO GP (PREVIOUSLY 500 CLASS) IS NOW FEARLESSLY TACKLING COMPETITION FROM FORMULA 1. THERE IS ALSO THE SUPERBIKE CATEGORY WITH LARGE ENGINE BIKES MADE FROM ROAD-GOING VEHICLES. IN ALL CATEGORIES, MANY ITALIAN DRIVERS ARE STILL PROTAGONISTS OF THE SPORT TODAY: ABOVE ALL VALENTINO ROSSI, WITHOUT FORGETTING CAPIROSSI, MELANDRI AND BIAGGI. MAKERS SUCH AS APRILIA AND DUCATI ARE CHALLENGING JAPANESE COMPANIES HONDA AND YAMAHA.

327 • Crazy two-wheel stunts: it is Travis Pastrana, here in the skies of San Francisco in 1999.

328-329 • Thomas Luethi on Honda during the trials of the Turkey 2005 GP, class 125.

330 ● The Spanish Pablo Nieto, winner of the Portugal 2003 GP, class 125, heads towards the box with his country's flag.

331 ● The British Michael Rutter on his Ducati 998, leaning over during the Macau 2003 GP, in China.

332 • The sequence of the fall of Tetsuya Harada during trials at the Phillip Island GP of Australia, class 500 in 2000.

333 • Thrown off his bike, Gabor Talmacsi flies off his KTM at the England 2005 GP class 125.

334 ● Angel Rodriguez loses control of his bike: it's the second round of trials at the Spanish GP of 2002 class 125.

334-335 ● Marco Simoncelli ended up rolling on the grass together with his Aprilia 125 during the Brazil GP trials 2004.

336 • The Japanese driver Youichi Ui on a Derbi 125 in the 2001 season: 16 Grand Prix disputed, 6 won.

337 • One of the motorcycling champions: here, Manuel Poggiali from San Marino is leaning with his knee grazing the tarmac.

338 • Daniel Pedrosa during the second round of trials at the England GP of 2006 valid for the GP.

338-339 • In a few meters a group of 125 drivers at the Italy GP of 2006 at the Mugello circuit: the group is led by Swiss Thomas Luethi.

Team mates seen wheel-to-wheel: they are Julian Simon and, behind, Stefan Bradl during the China 2006 GP trials.

342 ● A fall, without consequences, for Simoncelli at the Brazil 2004 class 125 trials.

342-343 ● Stefano Bianco falls from his Gilera and is avoided by Simone Corsi on his Honda: it is the Netherlands GP of 2003 class 125.

344 • Crouched low for maximum speed on his Aprilia 125, Alvaro Bautista is seen here at the Qatar GP of 8 April 2006.

345 • A brawl at the bend in the China GP class 125, on May 14 2006: leading the group is Hector Faubel, to come seventh at the finish.

346-347 • Passing under the crowd, this is Thomas Luethi on a Honda during the Germany 2006 GP class 125.

347 • Luethi bending again, but this time at the England GP of 2006 in Donington Park.

348-349 ● This landscape seems choreographed at the Spanish GP of 2006 class 125: leading is the local Alvaro Bautista.

349 ● "The doctor" Valentino Rossi during the qualifiers at the Qatar 2006 GP: he will start sixth.

350 • Leading the England GP, class 250, the Spanish Jorge Lorenzo who went on to win the race on his Aprilia on July 2nd 2006.

351 • Sandro Cortese, an Italo-German driver with the Caffe Latte team on a Honda 125, seen testing the Monmelo circuit, Catalunya, near Barcelona, on February 28th 2006.

352 • The Japanese 250 driver, Naoki Matsudo took off after touching with Czech Jakub Smrz at the Australia 2002 GP.

352-353 • Still trying to stay on his bike, this is Klaus Nohles at the Portugal 2004 GP trials, class 250.

354-355 • Frenchman Randy de Puniet at the Catalunya 2005 GP, class 250 on the Montmelo circuit near Barcellona.

355 • The final qualifying round at the Spanish GP of 2004: Makoto Tamada wearing number 6 leads the group.

356 • Still Honda 250 cc but another team, Repsol, and during 2006.

357 • A good omen was the sponsor Fortuna, with Honda for the 2004, 250 championship.

358 • Views of the 250 cc class at the Netherlands GP 2006: here is the Honda leaning into a bend.

359 • Ready as the driver to fold into a bend, this is a Yamaha 250 on the Dutch circuit of Assen.

360-361 • A gold and white livery recall the tobacco sponsor for this Aprilia 250 on the circuit of Assen in 2004.

362-363 ● A rumble in the Italy GP 2005 class 250: leading is the Spanish Daniel Pedrosa, who will win the race.

363 ● One of Valentino Rossi's classic gestures to celebrate victory: spinning in a circle on his bike: we're at the Spain 2004 GP.

364-365 ● Saluting after the finish line are Daniel Pedrosa on Honda, on the left, and Sebastian Porto, winner of the Netherlands GP 2005, class 250.

Anthony West bending on his KTM during the Netherlands GP in 2005, class 250 cc.

368 • Andrea Dovizioso on Honda 250 during trials at the circuit of Montmelo, Catalunya, near Barcellona, in March 2006.

369 • Alex Hofmann during the trials of the Japan 2006 GP on the Twin Ring circuit in Motegi.

370 • The Spanish Jorge Lorenzo on an
Aprilia racing in the Czech Republic GP
of 2006 in Brno, class 250: he will win.

370-371 • Lorenzo during qualifiers
at the Portugal GP of 2006 at Estoril.

On October 28th 2006, Hiroshi Aoyama races on the orange KTM during the test of the Valencian Community GP, class 250: he will gain pole position.

An accident involving Hiroshi Aoyama on KTM, on the right, and Alex Baldolini on an Aprilia in the first lap of the Italy 2006 GP.

376 • Sete Gibernau on Ducati hits the deck during the Catalunya 2006 round of the Moto GP with a series of falls.

377 • Shuhei Aoyama flew off his Honda in front of Roberto Locatelli after the start of the Turkey 2006 class 250 GP.

Hiroshi Aoyama on a KTM 250 cuts a trajectory across the bend in his home GP, that of Japan: it's 24 September 2006.

380-381 ● The unmistakable orange livery of the KTM bending during the Netherelands GP 2006, class 250.

381 ● Another KTM in Assen 2006 but this time it's the number 4 of the Japanese Hiroshi Aoyama.

382 • Sete Gibernau cuts a bend at the Czech GP of 2004: he will win the race in front of Valentino Rossi.

383 • Marco Melandri in front of Nicky Hayden: the Italian will win the 2005 Comunitat Valencia GP on the Ricardo Tormo track.

The blue livery of the Yamaha YZR-M1, 990 cc capacity, durign the GP 2004 championship.

386 • Japanese at the Moto GP: here, the Suzuki GSV-R which participated in the world championships of 2004.

387 • A blue livery again, but with different tones from the Yamaha and Suzuki, this is a Honda Rc211V partecipating in the Moto GP 2004.

The Honda Rc211V at the Moto GP 2004 has a yellow coat due to its sponsor.

● Valentino Rossi on Yamaha is glued to Sete Gibernau at the Spain 2004 GP: the Italian was to win.

392 • An unmistakable Valentino Rossi bending at the England GP in Donington Park: it's the 2004 championship.

393 • Rossi does his helmet up before embarking in the first session of trials on the Italy GP circuit of 2005.

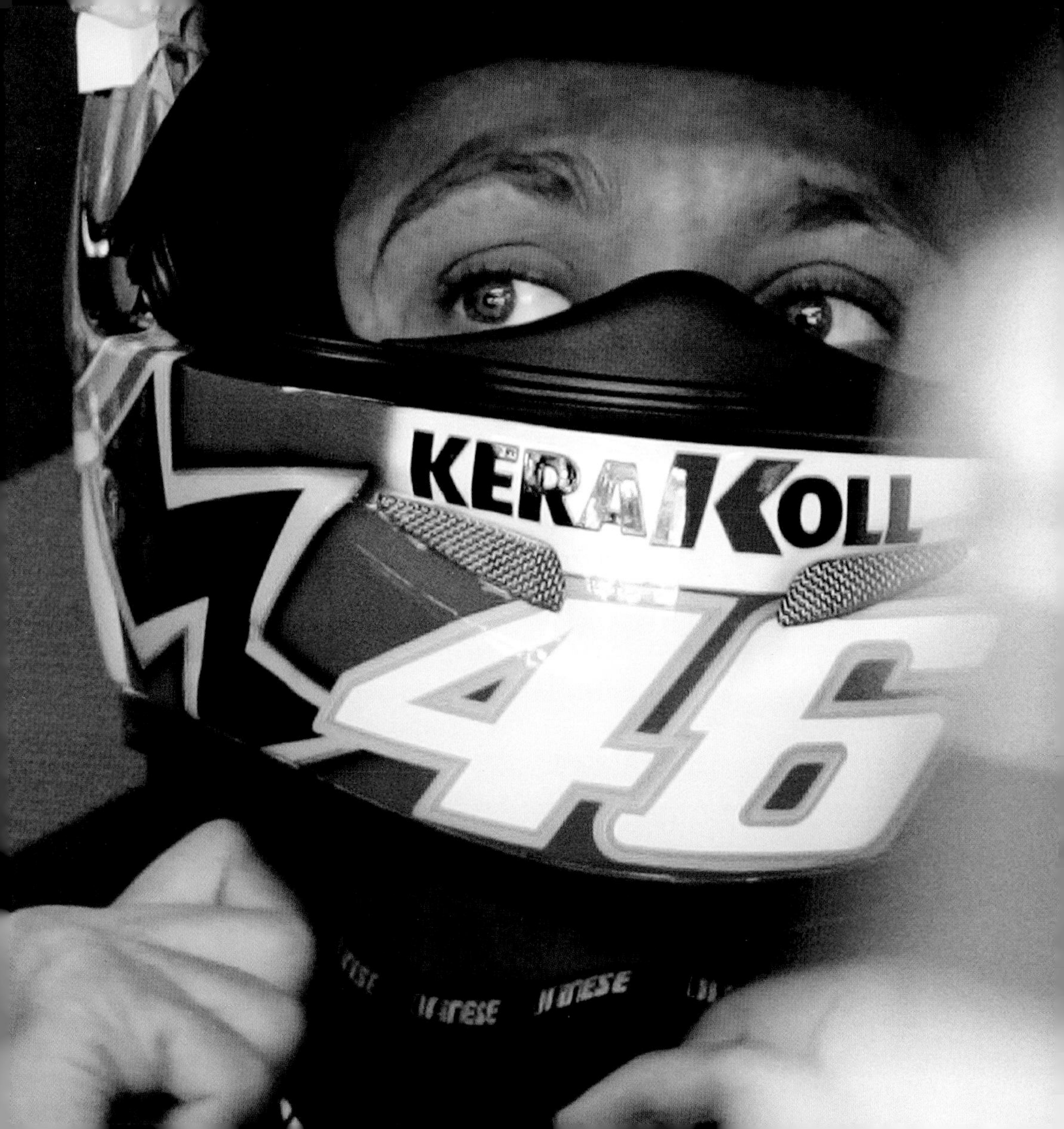
KERAKOLL
46

In these pages, there are some sequences of the spectacular flight of the Brazilian driver Alex Barros during the Australia GP trials of 2005 on Phillip Island, Melbourne.

396 ● Valentino Rossi on his Yamaha during trials at the China 2006 GP
on the Shangai circuit.

397 ● Rossi pulls a wheelie to celebrate his pole position on his Yamaha
at the Catalunya 2006 GP.

398-399 • Even from behind one easily recognizes Valentino Rossi, "The Doctor"; seen here at the Japan 2006 GP.

400-401 • Nicky Haiden on Honda is in front of James Ellison on his Yamaha during the GP trials at the Comunità Valenciana 2006.

402 • Valentino Rossi tackles the bend at the Portugal 2006 GP followed by Nicky Hayden on Honda.

403 • Quartet at the Mugello circuit chicane valid for the Italy 2006 GP: in the lead, Sete Gibernau on Ducati.

404-405 ● A green livery, the Kawasaki color: here the Zx-Rr during the 2006 Moto GP.

405 ● A white coat with red inserts for the Honda Rc211V at the 2006 Moto GP.

406-407 ● Marco Melandri's Honda overtakes on the inside at the Turkey 2006 GP and keeps Nicky Haiden at a distance.

Valentino Rossi celebrates with a few stunts for the pole positions obtained:
on the left in Spain 2006, at right at the Australia 2006 GP.

Marco Melandri, on the left, and Loris Capirossi collide at the first round of the Spain 2006 GP. The two end up on the track, involving other drivers too.

412 • Petter Solli on a Yamaha in the Superstock 2005: the Norwegian won his country's championship in 2004 and has a team of his own, Solli Racing.

413 • The Italian Ayrton Badovini competes in Superstock on his MV Agusta, a brand which brought him to victory after 30 years.

414 • The French driver Olivier Deporter on a Yamaha, leaning into a bend during a Superstock race in 2005.

415 • Again, Frenchman Deporter during acceleration, the front wheel lifting. He rides a Yamaha YZF-R1.

416 • A two-wheeled acrobat from San Francisco.

417 • Aerial trio at the Motocross Driver in Desert.

Some jump with their bikes, others are resigned to remain standing: motocross scenes in the desert.

420 • The US Drake McElroy during aerial performance during the Gravity Games of Cleveland in 2002.

420-421 • Analogous exhibition for Dustin Miller in the Freestyle section at the same Cleveland Gravity Games in 2002.

422 • Travis Pastrana performing for quite a crowd at the Los Angeles Memorial Coliseum Freestyle final: he will win the Gold.

423 • Ronnie Renner fighting for the title during the aerial final X-Games of Philadelphia 2002: he will come eighth out of seventeen.

424 • A sequence of an Indian Air Backflip at the Los Angeles X-Games of 2004: the net-less acrobat is Travis Pastrana.

425 • Pastrana flying at the Las Vegas Supercross of 2004.

Pastrana in aerial performance with leg acrobatics before a crowd.

428 • Jacky Vimond and his helmet are a mask of mud.

429 • Motocross class 250 cc race with the English driver Morris, on the right with bike 29.

430-431 • A speedway race where the drivers are always traveling horizontally: here are Joe Screen, on the left, and Joonas Kylmakorpi.

432 • A Derbyshire motocross event in England: a driver crosses a river at full speed.

433 • Spectacular image of a motocross race in Hurricane Mills, Tennessee (USA) in 2002.

A motorcross race just after the start, as seen by the drivers and bikes who are not yet muddy.

436 • Steam comes off the warm engine after the bike has crossed a river. We are in Hampshire, in England.

437 • He who stops is lost: here is a motocross racer in a bend with a lot of dirt in a Tennessee race (USA).

438 • Standing up on the bike without letting go of the gas to get out of the mush: motocross is often like this.

439 • A side to side fight for these two motocross drivers coming out of a bend.

440 • A speedway race on ice: notice the tires with nails to guarantee maximum grip.

441 • A moment of a speedway race on ice: the elliptical track leads the drivers to lean all the way around.

LEGENDARY
RACES

• Coming out of a dune at full speed. Never leave the gas, it could mean
the end of the race.

INTRODUCTION Legendary Races

It was not by chance that first competitions appeared as soon as motorbikes were invented. Initially they were held on the road, like they were for cars; for both vehicles the objective was to show that long journeys could be covered in far less time than with carriages. For both, the first test was the Paris-Bordeaux race of 1895, open to any motor vehicle. Today it would be hard to define the motorbikes, but two of them took part. The first race exclusively dedicated to motorbikes was held two years later across the channel. It was November 29th, 1897, and the competition took place in Richmond. (For the record, Jarriot won, beating Fournier.) Since then, motorbikes began their

INTRODUCTION

OWN EVOLUTION, FURTHER DISTINGUISHING THEMSELVES FROM CARS; THE LATTER WERE THE DOMAIN OF THE RICH AND WEALTHY, TRUE OBJECTS OF DESIRE, AND RARE ITEMS WITH EXORBITANT PRICES. MOTORCYCLES WERE INSTEAD ACCESSIBLE TO THE LESS WEALTHY MAN, BUT A WILDER AND BRAVER ONE: MORE ADVENTUROUS AND SPARTAN, FEELING AT ONE WITH HIS NEW RACEHORSE. LIKE THE SONS OF KING IXION OF GREEK MYTHOLOGY, HE WAS TO BECOME A CENTAUR. MOTORCYCLES SOON BECAME THE IDEAL MEANS FOR COMPETITION IN AUDACIOUS RACES (SUCH AS THE PARIS-VIENNA OF 1902 AND THE PARIS-MADRID OF THE FOLLOWING YEAR, WHICH WAS STOPPED AFTER THE FIRST LEG). AT THE BEGINNING OF THE 20TH CENTURY, THE FIRST EUROPEAN MOTORCYCLE FEDERATIONS WERE FOUNDED;

Legendary Races

Introduction

IN 1904 IN PARIS, THE INTERNATIONAL MOTORCYCLE FEDE-RATION WAS BORN (FIM). BUT ACROSS THE CHANNEL, THEY DIDN'T JUST STAND AND WATCH; ON MAY 28TH 1907, ON THE ISLE OF MAN, THE BIGGEST EUROPEAN MOTORCYCLE EVENT WAS HELD, TO THIS DAY CONSIDERED A CLASSIC: THE TOURIST TROPHY. THIS BECAME THE BACKBONE OF ALL MOTORCYCLE RACING. OVER THE YEARS, THE DIFFE-RENCES BETWEEN ROAD AND TRACK RACES GRADUALLY AROSE. TODAY ROAD RACES ARE CONSECRATED, ESPE-CIALLY IN THE PARIS-DAKAR, AN ENDURANCE RACE ALSO OPEN TO CARS, TRUCKS AND FOUR-WHEEL VEHICLES IN GENERAL–JUST LIKE THE PARIS-BORDEAUX.

• Drivers pushing their enduros into a gorge at the start of the 28th Enduro du Touquet, in northern France.

● Paris-Dakar: the group breaks up, drivers try to get away solo among the perils of the sand, surveyed by the helicopter. And after just one bend in the desert, the sand has risen and entered every crevice.

The public seeks privileged vantage points to see the racers speed by: scenes from Dakar 2006.

● Not only sand and dunes: one also encounters rocky tracts which cannot be allowed to slow the pace. Riders have to race many laps standing up on their bikes to keep their balance.

454 ● Frenchman Cyril Depres on a KTM LC4 690 exits these rocks: an ordinary scene at the Dakar race, here in 2007.

454-455 ● From the left, Czechs David Pabiska and Ivo Kastan on Yamaha and Suzuki in Dakar 2007. Taken between Er Rachidia and Ouarzazate.

456 • Spanish Marc Coma on a LC4 690 Repsol races solo in Er Rachidia during the Dakar.

456-457 • Sand on one side, the ocean on the other: the charming landscapes of the Paris-Dakar (here we see the Spanish Coma).

458-459 ●
This almost mystical image portrays Francois Vulliet on a Yamaha Action in Dakar 2007.

460-461 ● A crossing, one of the many along the Dakar route. And sometimes one crosses them together, in case of emergency.

The driver Repsol with the original bikes and orange suits of Dakar 2007 literally flying over dunes.

464-465 ● When getting off a
dune, one at a time, drivers are
extremely cautious; if a bike gets
stuck in the sand it's a problem.

465 ● A lonely racer during the
12th Paris-Dakar crossing the
Nigerian dunes.

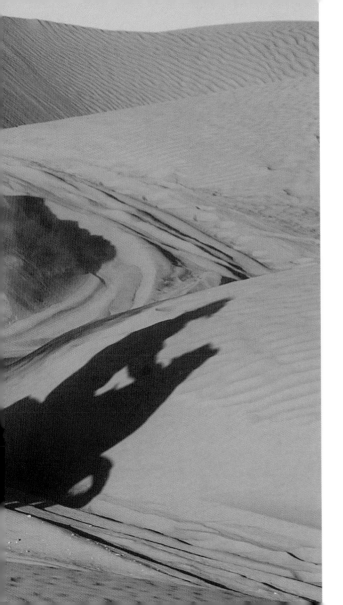

● The cleanest possible trajectory to avoid rolling and with only sand and more sand around.

468 • Giovanni Sala on a KTM 660 Rallye-Action in stage 9 of Dakar 2006 between Nouakchott and Kiffa.

469 • Difficult moments for this Repsol driver: the risk of getting stuck in the sand once and for good is close.

Like warriors, these drivers advance in parallel, taking on the sand and its snares.

472-473 • Motocross drivers at the start of the French Enduro du Touquet race. It attracts one thousand bikers and 300,000 spectators.

474-475 • An extreme fight between drivers who get to bite the sand: like grasshoppers they assault a dune in the Enduro du Touquet 2005.

476 • Skidding at the Enduro du Touquet 2005, the event created by Thierry Sabine, the inventor of the Paris-Dakar.

476-477 • Frenchman Aurelien Rebergues digs his Husqvarna out of the sand at the start of the 30th Enduro du Touquet.

A furious fight with falls in the gorge at the start of the Enduro du Touquet, the biggest motorcycle event in the wold.

A Driver and the Giza pyramids, in Cairo: it's the 10th Pharaohs Rally of 1991: Vatanen won for cars and LaPorte in the bike section.

The Italian driver Alberto Dottori falls during the first leg of the International Pharaohs Rally of 2004.

FREEDOM on WHEELS two

● The Vespa Piaggio in one of its most recent expressions–but always true to itself: the GTS.

INTRODUCTION Freedom on Two Wheels

These are the other half of the picture, more lighthearted, easier. For bikers with a capital B, scooters are not even considered motorcycles, because riders don't straddle the bike but merely sit on its seat. But if you think about it, it is thanks to this two-wheeler, loved by females and precious travel buddies for whizzing through chaotic city traffic, that the motorcycle market received a vital breath of fresh air between 1998 and 2000. In countries with many two-wheel vehicles, most bikes sold today are still scooters. Not only that, the boom of maxi-scooters has also re-launched traditional models; those drawn to higher en-

INTRODUCTION Freedom on Two Wheels

GINE CAPACITIES ARE ALSO MORE ATTRACTED TO CLASSIC MOTORBIKES. IN ANY CASE, THERE IS AB-SOLUTE ANTAGONISM BETWEEN MOTORCYCLISTS AND SCOOTER FANS; IT AS IF THEY WERE RIVAL FACTIONS, LIKE FERRARI AND PORSCHE LOVERS. IF YOU TALK ABOUT SCOOTERS, WHICH IS AN OLD TERM MEANING SKATE, THEN THE FIRST WAS THE VESPA. IT IS THE MOTHER OF THIS GENRE OF TWO-WHEEL VEHICLES, WHICH IS EASY TO DRIVE AND EASY TO REPAIR WITH-OUT GETTING YOUR CLOTHES DIRTY LIKE WITH TRADI-TIONAL MOTORBIKES. ALL SCOOTERS ARE ITS DESCEN-DANTS, AND THE VESPA HAS BECOME A WAY OF LIFE, IN ADDITION TO BEING A PHENOMENON IN THE WORLD MOTOR INDUSTRY AND ONE OF THE MOST GENIAL EN-

Freedom on Two Wheels
Introduction

GINEERING IDEAS IN HISTORY. THE VESPA IS AN ITALIAN PRODIGY, AN INDELIBLE SYMBOL OF MASS MOTORIZATION AND OF A PEOPLE'S DESIRE TO BE REBORN AFTER THE TRAGEDIES AND MISERY OF THE WAR. IT IS A SYMBOL OF FAMILY, OF WORK, AND OF THE FIRST WEEKENDS OUT OF THE CITY WITH A PICNIC HAMPER. IT IS AN IMAGE OF OPTIMISM, A RESERVED DISPLAY OF WEALTH, A SYMBOL OF LOVE FOR GENERATIONS OF YOUNG COUPLES. ALL THANKS TO ENRICO PIAGGIO, WHO FROM HIS DESIRE FOR INNOVATION GAVE US THIS *ENFANT PRODIGE*, AND TO THE AERONAUTICAL ENGINEER CORRADINO D'ASCANIO, THE INVENTOR OF THE VESPA.

• Revolutionary, it could be driver with no helmet but it was misunderstood: it's the BMW C1, here in its 1998 concept.

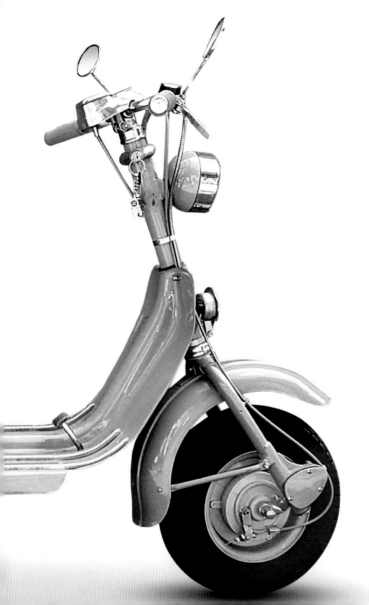

An icon of Italian-made scooters: this is the friendly Lambretta 125 of 1952.

● Trait d'union
between bikes and
scooters: this is the
Moto Guzzi Galletto of
the 50s with a leg
shield.

494 ● A variation on the Vespa Piaggio theme, with a famous name: it's the Paperino (Donald Duck), here from the front with its light on the wheel guard.

494-495 ● It's not just the color that makes the Paperino (Donald Duck) look like the famous animal: look at the covered back wheel.

Iso, known for the Isetta car, also made
a Scooter, looking like the Galletto
by Guzzi.

Another Italian variation on the
scooter theme: here is the Parilla,
a 50s model.

Essential, unmistakable and friendly: this is the Lambretta Innocenti, here in the C version of 1950.

● Along with the Vespa this was one of Italy's two-wheeled objects of desire: the Guzzi Galletto of 1958.

A version for connoisseurs, this is the Lambretta with a red seat: the 200X Special of 1966.

• A 70s version of the Vespa, here in a red livery: there is not really much difference from today's...

506 • Honda X8R-X is a scooter with small wheels, a high saddle, and a sporting carriage–and not only because of its vivacious colors.

507 • Very popular, especially among the fair sex, is the Aprilia Scarabeo 50 of 1994: it's practical and easy to handle.

• Metallic, chromed wing mirrors, handles and luggage rack, and double seat:
it's the Vespa LXV, from 50 to 185 cc

510 • Scooters with an urban inclination: it's a Honda Lead from 2003.

511 • More for touring and inclined to middle distance journeys, this is the Honda Foresight 2005: it is a so-called maxi scooter.

512 • The Koreans have also embarked in scooter production: among the most active is Kymco here with the Agi 50 4T R12 of 1987.

513 • The aggressive front of the Kymco Agility: like the other Koreans, it has an excellent quality/price ratio.

514 • The success of the Aprilia Scarabeo has brought the Noale production house to offer this 500 cc maxi version in 2002.

514-515 • The Honda Foresight, here in the 250 version of 1997, is one of the exponents of the maxi scooter boom of the late 90s.

One of the maxi scooters par excellence, with a motorcycle's capacity: this is the Suzuki Burgman 400, also designed for long journeys.

CUSTOM ART

- It's a shame to use it to travel seeing all its careful detail.
  But a custom can be like that.

INTRODUCTION Custom Art

Customized motorcycles are the means of travel as a way of escaping daily life and chasing after adventure. In popular imagery, custom bikes are the steel horses of Marlon Brando in "The Wild One" or Dennis Hopper in "Easy Rider," but little more. The days of the "On the Road" generation of rough riders, introverted and against the whole world, are no more; today's bikers are mature, serene people who generally try to avoid the stress of daily life, preferring to enjoy the pleasures of life and the world around them sitting on their favorite bike. Custom bikes fully satisfy this desire. The fad

INTRODUCTION Custom Art

WAS BORN IN THE USA OUT OF A WISH TO PERSONAL-
IZE BIKES ACCORDING TO ONE'S NEEDS AND TASTES,
MAKING EACH ONE UNIQUE IN DESIGN, IN ACCES-
SORIES AND IN CHOICE OF CHROME COMPONENTS.
THE MOST WELL-KNOWN BRAND IS HARLEY-DAVID-
SON, WHICH HAS GENERATED MANY CLONES. ONE
SHOULD NOT BE SURPRISED IF TWO BIKES OF THE
SAME BRAND AND MODEL ARE DIFFERENT; THEY AL-
LOW SO MANY POSSIBILITIES FOR CHANGING SO
MANY DETAILS THAT A MODEL EASILY BECOMES
UNIQUE. CUSTOM BIKES HAVE OTHER DIFFERENCES
DISTINGUISHING THEM FROM OTHERS: THE FRONT
WHEEL IS FURTHER FORWARD THAN THE HANDLE-
BARS, THE BACK WHEEL IS BIGGER THAN THE FRONT

Custom Art
Introduction

AND YOU SIT VERY LOW. THIS MAKES FOR A DRIVING POSTURE WHICH GIVES THE APPEARANCE OF GREAT COMFORT AS THE RIDER IS PRACTICALLY LYING ON HIS BACK, BUT IN TRUTH THIS POSITION IS QUITE TIRING AND NOT VERY AERODYNAMIC. HOLDING ONE'S ARMS HIGH AND WIDE UP WITH LEGS STRETCHED OUT IN FRONT IS CERTAINLY NOT THE BEST WAY TO COVER MILES AND MILES, RIDING FOR HOUR AFTER HOUR. OF COURSE, THESE BIKES ARE NOT MEANT FOR RACING AND COMPETITIVE SPEEDS ARE NOT THE GOAL. THE IMPORTANT THING IS TO HAVE A RELIABLE MOTOR THAT DOESN'T OVERHEAT AND NEVER BREAKS DOWN.

● Decisively patriotic, this is a Captain America II chopper of 2004, ready to cross the States.

- Few frills, just chrome
and a very urban gray.
No luggage or
passengers allowed.

A futuristic Custom Softail by Brouhard. See the shape of the handlebars and the back wheel with the mudguard acting as back rest.

A Harley in the clouds one could say, heady with the light and shiny colors of white and silver.

530 • The chopper is an American motorcycle icon used by riders for traveling.
Here in a soft version.

531 • It's called Special construction FXR Reptilian DNA and it's a very particular bike,
not only for the colors and decoration.

The Binford Money Shot
is a custom made in 2004
in a special brilliant green
enriched with colored
decoration.

Extreme and not only because of its back wheel, this Harley Davidson was customized by Jerry Covington.

Mick Jagger's signature, "Satisfaction" on the engine, photo tank and name changed to Harley Davidstones. Could it be unique?

- Iron Arrow is a very stylized
  concept chopper with a
  minimal tank.

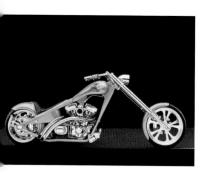

540 • A gold chassis for this custom which lives for looks.

540-541 • Another gold exercise, in this case with other decoration: all the rest is chrome.

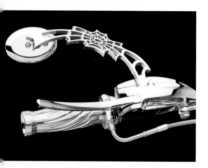

542 ● The chrome detail
of the handle and wing-mirror
with spiderweb motif: here
personalization is at a peak.

542-543 ● Bam/Ink made
this 2004 chopper in a
kaleidoscope of color and
with its particular exhausts.

Sinuous lines and plays on curves for this chopper with carioca colors made in 2006 by Reneck Engineering.

Refined tones but
very practical and ready
for long journeys;
a 2006 Prostreet.

This custom made in 2003 could be defined a design model, with its flying lines and original copper color.

In these pages two choppers on the theme of lizard green: the model on the left has a long saddle, though.

552 • Cutting-edge custom bikes, aggressive and furtive like this are made by
Jerry Covington, a recognized master on the scene since the legendary 70s.

553 • The exclusivity of a product can be seen in the minutest detail, as shown
by this Jerry Covington tank, with sober and cutting tribal motifs.

554 ● Custom motorcycles often become the canvas where colors are expressed best in personal and original fantasies.

555 ● There's also room for details besides personalized colors: this is the case for this chromed air filter cover.

● An eccentric color and eye-catching handlebars, as if to compensate the bareness of the front.

558 • A refined pearl white characterizes this Brouhard custom softail of 2005.

558-559 • The rear of this white steel horse: notice the barbed wire on the tank and wheel guards.

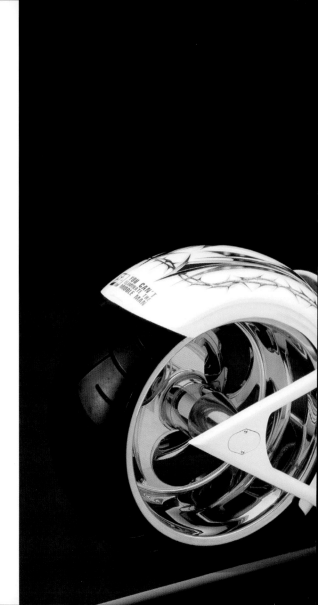

The thief comes only to steal
and kill and destroy. I have come
that they may have life,
and have it to the full.
John 10:10

With the colors of steel, this custom Harley is dedicated to the Blues Brothers and to blues in general.

562 • A chromed chassis and sophisticated foot rest for this very elegantly colored custom.

562-563 • An all-curve custom with overall harmony only upset by the big exhaust.

564 • There's also room for a leather side
bag on this original custom called Bombshell.

565 ● The side of the Bombshell: the seat
is reminiscent of a bicycle's.

566 • An exaggerated chopper with a chassis which recalls the colors of the sky: the designer tank implies little autonomy.

566-567 • The side view of a chopper: two can ride with a truly original rest for the passenger.

568 • Particularly refined decor for this shiny chopper which offers a very comfortable driving place, arms excluded.

569 • A detail of the seat and the back: here the theme is blue jeans.

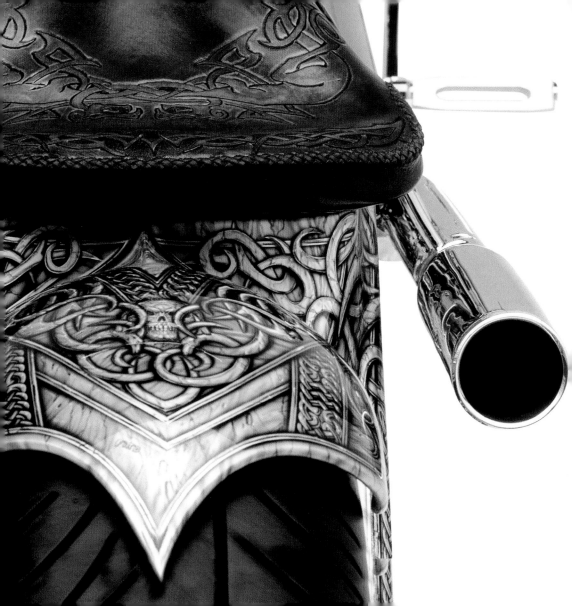

- Room for the flames for this custom based on shades of blue, with a very small handlebar.

A very long custom for two with articulated chassis elements to support the large dimensions.

The tank up high, imposing fork, very low seat; on this F. Rod custom by Rodlin, green like its chassis, you practically sit on the back wheel.

576 ● An upsetting tank for this blood
colored custom, softened by the
beige seat.

576-577 ● A long saddle for two,
the passenger practically on the large
back wheel.

578 • Rather than a chopper it's an exercise of style to emphasize some elements such as the handlebar and front chassis trellis.

579 • The detail of the intake tubes with their grill at the height of the seat.

580-581 • Attention-grabbing and exaggerated chrome with gold inserts, this bike has details worthy of a limousine, like the soft seat.

581 • This very long custom privileges corners rather than sinuous lines.

582 • A complete fairing and a clear homage to Pepsi Cola. An unusual custom which seems not to have wheels.

583 • Another interpretation of the fairing: here the dominant theme is red, a homage to aerodynamics.

584 • A 1992 custom by
FLH with its mission in the
background: long journeys.

584-585 • A long Harley
Davidson which wouldn't look
bad on the race track.

● A very refined configuration including the studded seat for this chopper with a generous behind.

588 • This simply black custom looks like an assembled bike only making allowances for chromed mechanics.

589 • The detail of the refined cooling wind of the cylinders.

This Silverado custom doesn't even look painted. The colors of the steel pay homage to women and gambling.

● The lights of the studio where it was photographed generate interesting reflections from this custom with an elegant black livery.

594 ● A bizarre line and extravagant tank for this chopper with a very simple seat.

595 ● The detail of the drawing which decorates the end part of the back mudguard.

The front wheel seems almost detached from the rest of this custom with a very refined chassis and mechanical arrangement.

598 • Elegant, with kind colors and sober decorations, this custom is characterized by a female presence on the tank (Glamour Girl) and a pink seat.

599 • Glamour Girl details: notice the drawings and inserts even on the motor.

600 • A very special custom which denotes the craftwork of its hand-made construction.

600-601 • Refined chrome and mechanics are the DNA of this custom.

602 • Made in Texas in 2003, this red chopper has flames along its whole body.

603 • It's called a Swift Barchopper Csf and it dates back to 2002: notice the refined spokes of the alloy wheels.

● Gold and silver for
this custom with refined
details even in the livery
of the wheels.

A homage to aerodynamics with a complete fairing for the back wheel and large footboards.

A work of Futurism on two wheels: how else to judge this Thunder Mountain Motor Sports Sinful of 2005?

610-611 • The custom concept is very stylized here: the original lines and clean chroming are privileged.

612-613 • There had to be a homage to James Dean, a very restrained but elegant custom.

This motorcycle seems to have come out of a science fiction movie and has good aerodynamics.

616 • A little custom, a little racy:
this is the trademark of the
Battistini Special.

616-617 • A D'antan custom, this
is a Ness Stalgia which seems to
have borrowed some parts from
a Cadillac Eldorado.

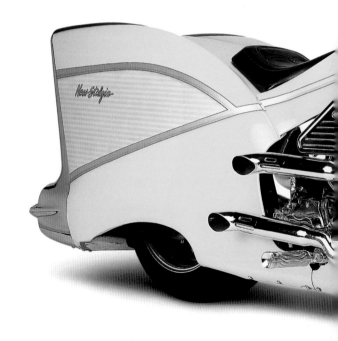

● A style exercise concentrating on the detail of the chrome and decorations. Very refined detailed set-up, like the decorative element which concludes the posterior of this custom.

620 • Aggressive handlebars and back wheel for this sporty custom of 2003.

621 • Athletic and with very particular chroming, (defined kryptonite green)
this is a Sick chopper of 2004.

● Good-looking but not exaggerated, this custom wants to draw attention to the posterior, an often neglected "area" on bikes.

● Brazilian tones with flames for this typically US chopper of 2004.

626-627 • What can be said of this tiger on two wheels that even has a tail at the back? Simply delightful!

628-629 • This model would get compliments from Count Dracula...

ON THE
ROAD

- In India this is how the problem of congested city traffic is solved: traveling by four on a motorbike.

INTRODUCTION On the Road

THERE IS NO TRACK, NO RACE, NO PODIUM. THE COURSE IS THE WORLD. THE ADVERSARY IS NATURE, WITH THE SPIRIT OF ADVENTURE AND PASSION BEING THE FORCES THAT ARE RELEASED BY THE DESIRE TO EXPLORE AND FACE THE CHALLENGE OF HUGE DISTANCES, PROVIDED THAT EACH RIDES HIS OWN BIKE, THE SAME NO-FRILLS ONE THAT ALSO TAKES HIM TO WORK. CALL THEM RAIDS, JOURNEYS, OR TOURS, WHOEVER HAS GOTTEN ON A BIKE FROM THE DESIRE FOR FINDING OUT WHAT IS OUT THERE, BEYOND DAILY LIFE, TRAVELING 100 OR 100,000 MILES, HAS GIVEN AN OUTLET TO THAT HUMAN WISH TO TRAVEL FAR, TO FIND OUT WHAT IS AROUND EVERY BEND, CHALLENGING THEMSELVES OUT OF A THIRST FOR KNOWLEDGE AND TO DIS-

INTRODUCTION On the Road

COVER ONE'S OWN LIMITS AS WELL AS THOSE OF THE MACHINE. A WORLD TOUR IS OBVIOUSLY THE ULTIMATE EXPERIENCE, BUT THE SAME SPIRIT ACCOMPANIES A SUNDAY OUTING, A WEEKEND TRIP OR HOLIDAY TOUR. THE IMPORTANT THING IS TO TRAVEL, BUT WITH THE BIKE AND ITS RITUAL: THE PREPARATION OF THE MA-CHINE, THE LOADING OF ESSENTIAL AND ADEQUATE BAGGAGE WITH THE NECESSARY COVERINGS, A TENT AND THE TOOLS FOR QUICK REPAIRS. IF THE JOURNEY IS A STORY WORTH TELLING, THEN ALL THE BETTER. LIKE THOSE TAKEN ON BOARD VESPA SCOOTERS: YES, THAT'S RIGHT, NOT MOTORBIKES MADE FOR GREAT JOURNEYS LIKE CUSTOM VERSIONS OR MODELS WHICH REACH THE SPEED OF SOUND, BUT ON THE SCOOTER

On the Road

Introduction

THAT DEFINES THE GENRE, CAPABLE OF RUNNING THOUSANDS OF MILES ON ROADS OF ALL KINDS, FROM ROME TO SAIGON, FROM MELBOURNE TO CAPE TOWN, FROM ALASKA TO THE TIERRA DEL FUEGO, FROM ATHENS TO THE NORTH POLE. TRIPS TAKEN BY UN-TRAINED RIDERS, WITHOUT ITINERARIES AND WITHOUT SPONSORS, STORIES OF GLOBE TROTTING TO MAKE EVEN THE LAZIEST SIT UP IN THEIR CHAIRS. IT DOESN'T MATTER HOW MUCH TIME IT TAKES, SOMETIMES YEARS. BUT THOSE WHO VOW EVERLASTING LOVE TO THE TWO WHEELS SHARE THE BEST YEARS OF THEIR LIVES WITH THEM.

• Cyclists at the Sturgis Rally 2006 as they ride the curves of the Iron Mountain Road in the United States.

636 • There is a lot of national pride in Don Ackerman, famous biker photographed along the highway of the 2006 Sturgis Rally.

637 • Huge group of Harleys parked side by side on the road in Monument Valley, Utah.

638-639 • Gathering of bikers at the starting point of the Sturgis Rally in South Dakota: every year there are more than half a million participants.

639 • Scenes from the Sturgis Rally: ones passes a row of hundreds of parked bikes before finding a parking spot.

A group of bikers in Rochford, South Dakota (population 25 and a saloon, at the foot of the Black Hills), sets off for the Sturgis Motorcycle Rally.

● Ducati motorcycle rally
in Misano Adriatico (Rimini),
in Italy: there are thousands
at the starting point.

Motorcycle abundance in front of the Roslyn Cafè in Washington State, USA.

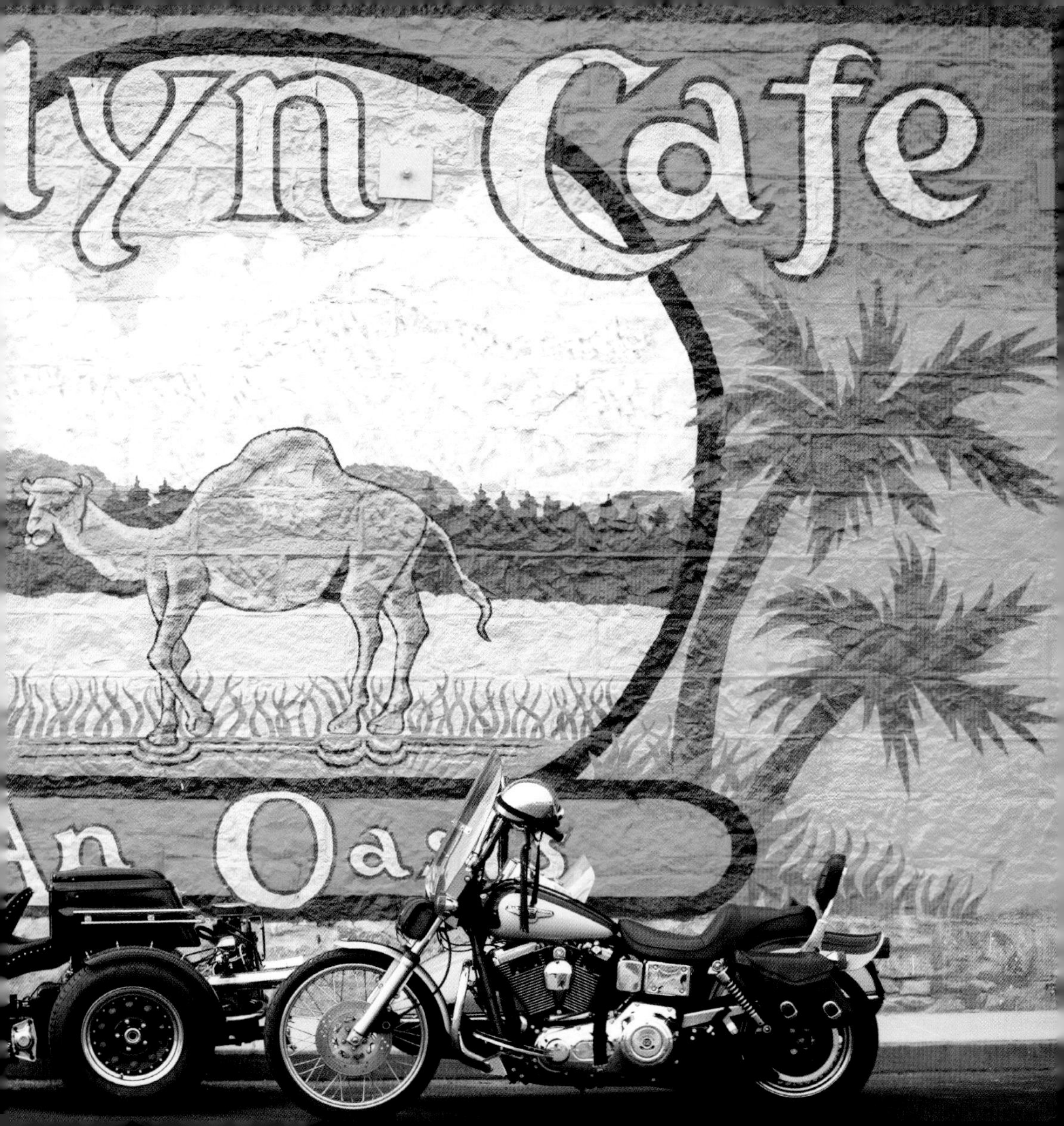
lyn Cafe
n Oas

646-647 • Navajo
bikers traveling the
roads of Arizona, in the
United States.

648-649 • Congested
traffic on two wheels, in
Ho Chi Minh City,
Vietnam: all on
motorbikes, none
wearing a helmet.

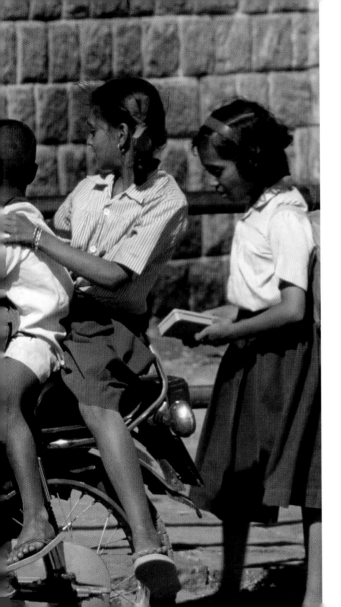

In India, it is normal to carry an entire family on a motorcycle. Nevertheless, accidents are less frequent than one would expect.

None strays far from his bike, even while praying: 1982 in Nigeria, at the Kano mosque.

654 • Few cars and many scooters during rush hour in the streets of Hanoi in Vietnam.

655 • Fine example of loading (or balance) for this boy's bike in the traffic of Bangkok, Thailand.

● Vietnamese newlyweds on a scooter, with the bride in "traditional" dress with bouquet seated sideways.

658 • In Can Tho, in Vietnam, produce vendors in the 90's used the motorcycle seat.

659 • A difficult balancing act for this Vietnamese boy transporting soccer balls.

● Even nomad shepherds in northern China no longer use Mongol horses, but off-road bikes. Here we are on Karakul Lake, at the base of the Mustaghata mountains (25,000 feet high).

662 • Traveling in more than two on a motorcycle is limitless: here we are in Tinerhir, in Morocco.

663 • Mongolian family on a Sunday trip in Undursant. On a motorcycle, naturally, even with four of them.

664 • Milk transport in Rajasthan, India. Naturally on a bike.

665 • Incredible hauling test for this bike in the province of Takeo in Cambodia.

COLORS
MOTION
in

- Hot chroming on this custom bike, where the plating acts as a backdrop for the skull.

INTRODUCTION Colors in Motion

Gas tanks can mean much more than simple personalization or the desire to distinguish one's bike from others. They represent a lifestyle, and are a way of communicating through the only part of the vehicle that can do this. The gas tank becomes a surface on which to write, draw, depict or portray the biker's lifestyle. Should you think that this is a rare phenomenon among some lost tribe of bikers, you would be wrong. Just have a look on the internet and google "tank painters" and you will get more than 680,000 hits. Not very many? Well, consider that each result opens a universe of illustrators and air-brush artists,

INTRODUCTION Colors in Motion

MODERN DECORATORS OF THE THIRD MILLENNIUM SPREAD ALL OVER THE GLOBE AND SPEAKING THE UNIVERSAL LANGUAGE OF BIKERS, USING THE ROUNDNESS AND SHAPE OF TANKS LIKE A CANVAS ON WHICH TO MAKE *BONA FIDE* WORKS OF MOVING ART. FUNDAMENTALLY, THE MOTORBIKE ITSELF IS AN ARTWORK IN MOVEMENT AND HAS BEEN THE OBJECT OF MUCH CREATIVE EFFORT BY PAINTERS AND SCULPTORS ON ALL CONTINENTS. IN THE CASE OF TANK PAINTERS, IT BECOMES EVEN MORE PERSONAL; THEY GENERALLY EXPRESS THEMSELVES ON TANKS BUT CAN USE THE ENGINE AND VALVE COVERS OR EVEN THE HELMET AS WELL. IN ANY CASE, THE TANK IS THE MAIN ELEMENT, COLD AND METALLIC IN FRONT OF THE SEAT, ALWAYS

Colors in Motion
Introduction

IN FRONT OF THE SEATED BIKERS SO THAT THEY CAN KEEP IT UNDER CONTROL. IT BECOMES A SHOWPIECE OF LANDSCAPES, WRAP-AROUND FEMALE FIGURES, EPIC CHARACTERS AND SPECTRAL FIGURES, AS IF THEY WERE TATTOOS, LIKE THE ONES ON THEIR OWNER'S BODY. THEY ARE INDELIBLE MARKS FOR THE ON-THE-ROAD WAY OF LIFE, TO BE SHOWN TO THE PEOPLE YOU MEET TO CREATE A SENSE OF BELONGING. OFTEN THEY BEAR THE SIGNS OF THE DUST WHICH THE BIKE AND RIDER HAVE ACCUMULATED ALONG THE THOUSANDS OF MILES DEVOURED ON THE ROAD OF THE WORLD.

- More than a decoration, it's a lifestyle, right down to the engine. Harley Davidson style.

● The rider and his ghostly shadow; not just decoration, it is an autobiographical work of art.

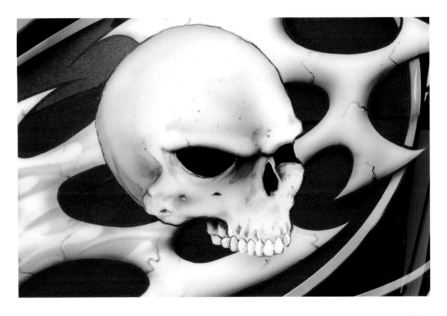

674 ● A very simple skull minus the jaw stands out on the gas tank of this custom bike.

675 ● A parade of decorated bikes: bright colors and images of death
the common themes.

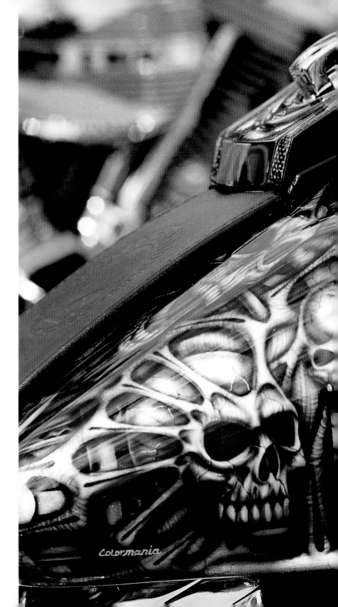

Death in its many forms, in an evocative three-dimensional effect thanks to the chrome-plated gas tank.

● Somber tones
and a skull with hat
characterize this
gas tank.

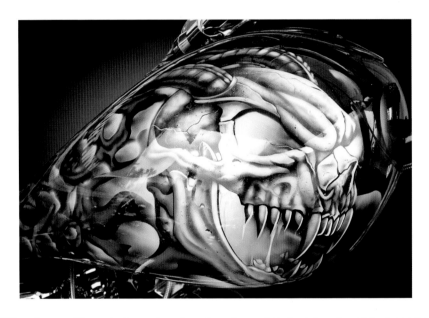

680 • An unsettling satanic creature from the afterworld is the leitmotiv of this decoration.

681 • This skull emerging from the American flag was immortalized at a convention at Daytona Beach.

682-683 • Heavenly colors form the background to this demon, an image both ironic and mocking.

684 • For the person who decorated this gas tank, biking is like poker.

684-685 • Same bike, seen from the side: the references to gambling are clear. With the obligatory pin-up.

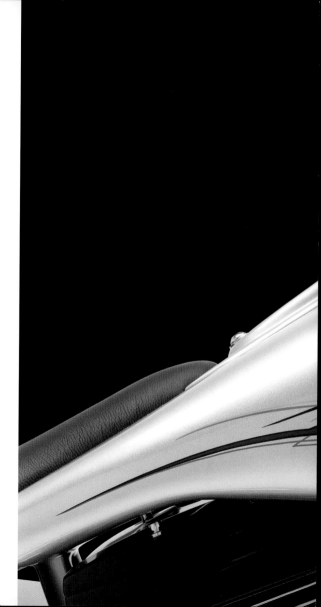

- The female figure, often exaggerated, is the star of many gas tanks.

688 • Generous curves, come-hither stares: the teardrop shape of the gas tanks favors the feminine form.

689 • Nautical inspiration for this gas tank, with a sexy girl leaning on the porthole.

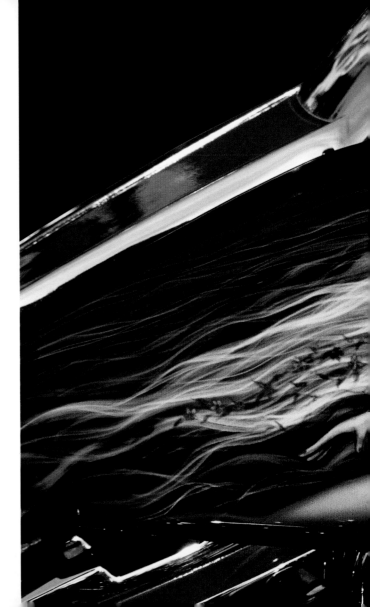

- The wind whips through their hair at high speeds. The result? A very artistic decoration.

- A Native American
inspired the author of
this hot-toned
decoration.

694 • A skull and a female figure coexist in eye range of the rider.

695 • A bawdy scene of sea creatures swimming in the depths on the sides of a black gas tank.

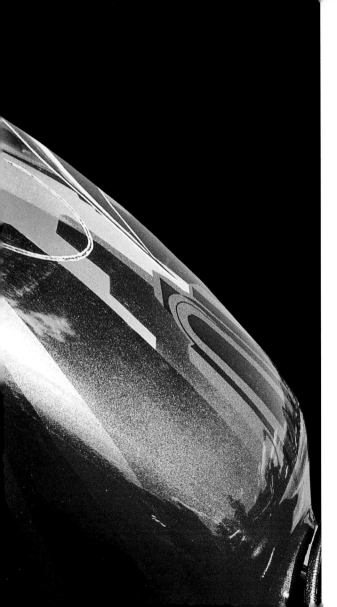

696-697 ● Splendid chromatic execution of this decoration on the theme of a woman's face.

698-699 ● There's also room for superheroes: here, an attractive Cat Woman of uncertain intentions.

● The gas tank of this
custom bike is like
a science fiction
cartoon, with the
hero who protects
the weak.

Italian-style romance for bikers in love: "Baci" chocolates deserve a decoration.

The theme of travel is dear to the iconography of Harley Davidson and in general to motorcycles dedicated to long trips.

706 • Delicate colors and South
American themes adorn this
motorcycle.

706-707 • Original theme, bright
colors: this bike will surely not go
unnoticed.

In this interpretation of the subject of travel, the scene is of an airplane of decidedly rapacious appearance.

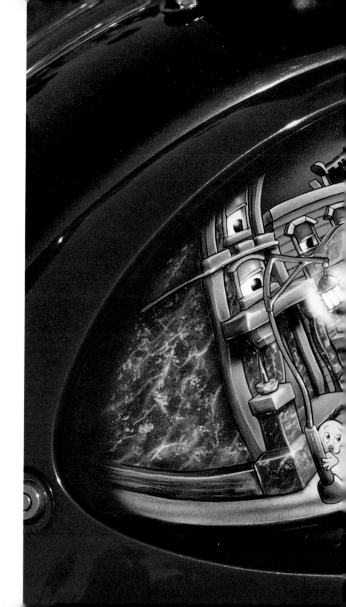

Cute and fun, a parade of Warner Bros. cartoon characters.

Two gods on a single tank: one apparently human, the other stamped with a trademark.

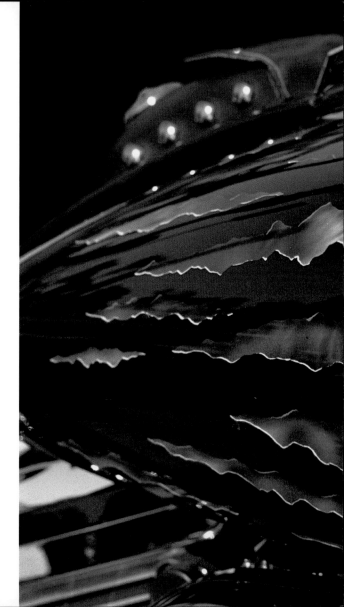

There is no lack of animals on gas tanks, who merit respect because they inspire fear.

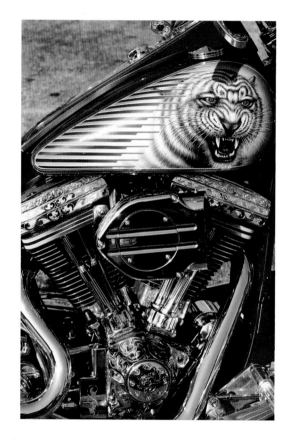

716 • This tiger shares the spotlight with decorations along with chrome plating and engraving on the engine.

717 • Scenes from life in the forest: the imagination in the decoration is limitless.

718-719 • Colors in warm orange tones frame a Samson who breaks out from the gas tank.

720 • The need for freedom and the show of strength are well-represented by the eagle on this Harley Davidson.

720-721 • Dragons, flames and fantastic creatures are often the decorative theme on gas tanks.

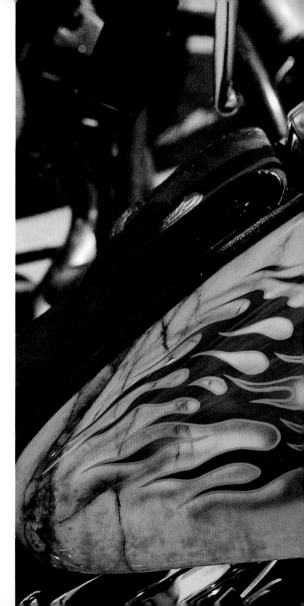

722 • Gods represented by wild female figures astride winged horses.

723 • Dragons and Vikings for this bike: the flat form and dimensions of the gas tank are ideal for this type of representation.

724-725 ● More dragons and devilish creatures in the shape of the gas tank: they inspire fear and respect like the biker.

726-727 ● There is even a title (Alien) for this gloomy science-fiction decoration.

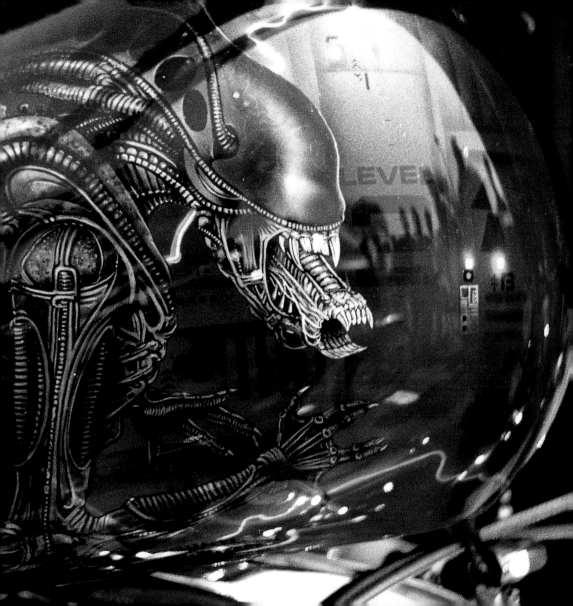

AUTHORS Biographies

■ **VALERIA MANFERTO DE FABIANIS**

She is the editor of the series. Valeria Manferto De Fabianis was born in Vercelli, Italy and studied arts at the Università Cattolica del Sacro Cuore in Milan, graduating with a degree in philosophy.

She is an enthusiastic traveler and nature lover. She has collaborated on the production of television documentaries and articles for the most prestigious Italian specialty magazines and has also written many photography books.

She co-founded Edizioni White Star in 1984 with Marcello Bertinetti and is the editorial director.

■ **ENZO RIZZO**, professional journalist, is Vice-Director of *Monsieur* and *Spirito di Vino* magazines, writes for the newspaper *Il Giornale* and for *Flotte & Finanza* magazine. He has written about automobiles since 1992 and is a member of the Italian Automobile Journalists Union. He began his career as a writer for *Guida*. In 1994 he was with *Autolink News*, then in 1995 he went to trade publications *Radar-Monovolume & Station Wagon* and *Radar- Coupe & Spider*.

Between 1998 and 2001 he was the editor of *Class and Gentleman* and until 2001 edited the automobile sections of *Campus*, *Case & Country* and *Classcity*, and until 2003 those of *Milano Finanza* and *Italia Oggi*. From 2004 to 2005 he wrote the automobile column for *Finanza & Mercati*, *Borsa & Finanza*, and *Tuttofondi/Freetime*. Along with colleague Giuseppe Guzzardi he is the author of the multimedia work *Alfa Romeo, A Century of Racing* (1997), and of the books of *Cabriolet* (1998) and *100 Years of Auto Racing* (1999) published by White Star, the publisher for whom in 2006 he wrote the title *Automobiles* for the Cubebook series.

INDEX

INDEX

PHOTO CREDITS

PHOTO CREDITS

Proframe Photography: pages 356, 357, 358, 359, 360-361, 366-367, 380-381, 381, 384-385, 386, 387, 388-389, 404-405, 405, 412, 413, 414, 415, 430-431

Steve Raymer/Corbis: page 659

Joao Relvas/epa/Corbis: pages 370-371, 402

Royalty Free/Corbis: page 417

Rue Des Archives: pages 47, 165 (Motocycles Cottereau et Cie © Rene Vincent, by SIAE 2007), 170

Albert Saladini: pages 2-3, 18-19, 30-31, 34-35, 41, 52-53, 54-55, 138-139, 242-243, 244-245, 574, 575, 582-583, 583, 614-615, 626-627, 628-629, 671, 672-673, 675, 676-677, 688, 689, 690-691, 696-697, 698-699, 700-701, 704-705, 708-709, 710-711, 712-713, 714-715, 716, 717, 718-719, 720, 720-721, 724-725, 726-727

Frank Sander/Thunder Media Service: pages 16-17

Howard Sayer/Alamy: page 392

Ferdinando Scianna/MagnumPhotos/ Contrasto: pages 642, 642-643

Tim Shaffer/Reuters/Contrasto: page 423

Filip Singer/epa/Corbis: page 370

Richard Smith/Corbis: page 432

SuperStock/Agefotostock/Marka: page 438

Suzuki motor corporation: pages 185, 234, 272-273, 308-309, 310-311, 312-313, 314, 314-315, 316-317, 516-517

Swim Ink2, LLC/Corbis: pages 146, 148, 149, 154

Travelstock44/Alamy: page 654

Ufficio Stampa Gruppo Piaggio: pages 336, 337, 484

Ufficio Stampa Moto Guzzi: pages 57, 64-65, 65, 104-105, 296-297

UPPA/Photoshot Photo: page 489

www.vajenti.com: pages 196, 197, 204-205

Robert van der Hilst/Corbis: page 662

Visual Arts Library (London)/Alamy: pages 150-151

Patrick Ward/Corbis: pages 436, 681, 692-693, 694, 695

David H. Wells/Agefotostock/Marka: pages 631, 664

Nick Wheeler/Corbis: page 663

www.honda4fun.com: pages 124-125

Michael Yamashita/Corbis: page 658

Bobby Yip/Reuters/Contrasto: page 331

Giuliano Zanetti and Matteo Nanni: pages 70-71, 74, 74-75, 76-77, 78-79, 80, 320-321, 500-501

Cover: Marvy!/Corbis

Back cover: Edisport Editoriale, archivio rivista Motociclismo

The aerographies shown on pages 722 and 723 have been realized by Simona Trozzi, website www.simonatrozzi.it

The Publisher would like to thank:

Suzuki Italia, the MV Agusta Press Office, Dr. Sergio Vicarelli and Gian Paolo Cerizza, Daniele Torresan, Ducati Motor Holding S.p.a, the Piaggio Foundation and the Piaggio Historical Archives

It's true, Vespa is the definition of scooter, but the Lambretta can also be considered an icon: here is the Model D from 1952.

Cover • Custom Harley Davidson, 1997.

Back cover • Vespa Piaggio, 2001.